ADULT CHILDREN RAISING CHILDREN

Sparing Your Child
From Co-dependency —
Without Being Perfect Yourself

Randy Colton Rolfe

Health Communications, Inc.
Deerfield Beach, Florida

Randy Colton Rolfe
Newtown Square, Pennsylvania

Library of Congress Cataloging-in-Publication Data

Rolfe, Randy Colton
    Adult children raising children : sparing your child from co-
  dependency — without being perfect yourself / by Randy Colton Rolfe.
       p.   cm.
    Includes bibliographical references.
    ISBN 1-55874-055-4 : $8.95
     1. Parenting—United States.   2. Co-dependence (Psychology)
  I. Title.
  HQ755.8.RR64   1989   89-36007
  649'.1—dc20   CIP

© 1990 Randy Colton Rolfe

ISBN 1-55874-055-4

Publisher: Health Communications, Inc.
          3201 S.W. 15th Street
          Deerfield Beach, FL 33442-8124

Cover design by Vicki Sarasohn

Dedication

I dedicate this book with love
to my beloved families, old and new,
and to all those who seek a richer family life.

Acknowledgments

I would like to acknowledge the help and inspiration of the following people: my husband, my son, my daughter and my mother; my mentors, editors and friends, including Frank, Paul, Mickey, Gary, Peter, Leslie, John, Helen, Ken, William, Karen, Lorraine, Germaine, Dick, Richard, Leonore, June, Rokelle, Janet, Susan, Sharon, Rebecca, Susie, Owen, Perry, Wayne, Rich, Mary Ellen, Gail, Pam, Don and Ruth; my students in my *Parenting Today* and *Personal Best* seminars; and the many others who have supported me in so many different ways in writing this book. I thank you all.

Contents

Caught In The Middle — The Special Challenge

1

Over 34 million Americans had a parent who was dependent on alcohol or other mood-altering chemical. A good proportion of these have their own children now.

In the last decade, millions of adults have recognized the lingering co-dependent attitudes and reactions that this environment engendered and have found hope in identifying themselves as adult children of alcoholics or addiction (ACoAs).

Al-Anon groups, for the families of alcoholics, have seen a great increase in the proportion of their membership that these adult children represent. And groups specifically for adult children of alcoholics have sprung up all over the country to accommodate their special needs.

Many have helped these adult children to identify themselves, including knowledgeable therapists, family counselors trained in addiction, anonymous self-help groups on the Al-Anon model, and authors like Janet Woititz with *Adult Children Of Alcoholics* and Melody Beattie with *Co-dependent No More*.

Meanwhile, Americans are seeking guidance as never before on parenting issues. In recent years, many young adults have put off child-rearing until after they have established careers. The baby-boom generation only recently reached its delayed birthing peak, yielding in 1988 the most babies born in 25 years.

When these women and men do have their children, they approach parenting more consciously and with greater effort than ever before to prepare themselves, through reading, education, advice and introspection.

Other parents began parenting in younger years, without as much thought. They identify with the label *Adult Children* in a different way. They feel that in too many ways they were still children when they began raising children. They struggle now with guilt over what they wish now that they had known then.

In my seminars and counseling around the country on parenting issues, I have met thousands of parents who are aware of alcohol dependency or other addiction in their childhood home. Most are confident they have licked the statistical chances that dependency might appear in their new home. But they fear that the cycle of co-dependency will continue.

They want new tools and information to help them weed out the troublesome attitudes and behaviors that they still carry. They want to raise their children to be independent, happy people, even if they themselves don't feel quite there yet. And they want to feel confident and proud of themselves as parents.

This book speaks to them, to you. It draws on real life experience with one of the toughest issues of our time to show you how, as an adult child raising children, you can spare your children from co-dependency without being perfect yourself.

A Special Challenge For
Adult Children Raising Children

Adult children raising children face a special parenting challenge because of one dramatic conflict. They are caught in the middle between two opposing messages about their own self-worth.

On the one hand, they remember and hold on to messages of low self-worth from their family of origin, either from guilt they assumed for the troubles at home or from continuous parental criticism of their basic competence and motives.

On the other hand, they long to believe the new messages of high self-worth from their children, as they experience the natural love and awe in which their children hold them as parents.

This conflict between messages can make you feel ambivalent, torn, angry, helpless, cynical, depressed, inconsistent and indecisive. It can also restimulate the reactive devices that you developed in the conflicted training ground of your childhood home.

Mixed messages you may be giving your children now as a result can recreate for them the same forces with which you were raised, even without any addiction in your new family.

You can end this cycle of co-dependency for you and your children now. Get to know your feelings and where they come from. Find out what mistaken conclusions you drew from your childhood experience. And replace them with interpretations and affirmations grounded in spiritual reality, so as to empower yourself to become the parent you want most to be.

The Emperor's New Clothes

According to a fairy tale, an emperor wanted a new majestic robe and sent for a special tailor. For an incredible sum, the tailor promised to make a robe that surpassed all others: It would help the emperor discover whom he could trust.

The emperor was excited and appeared promptly for his fitting. The tailor explained the secret of the robe: Only the righteous could see it.

The emperor saw nothing, but knowing he had not always been righteous, he said nothing. He held out his arms and let the tailor drape the robe. He looked in the mirror, saw only his royal underwear, but still said nothing.

He paid the tailor as agreed and looked forward to testing his courtiers' honesty the next day. When all were assembled, the emperor made his entrance. A gasp rushed through the great hall. No one said a word. Each courtier paid his respects and gave his compliments, as they knew the emperor wished.

All except a little child. Peeking out from behind his courtier father's robe, he pointed at the emperor and giggled. Stepping forward, he declared, "Father, His Majesty has no robe!"

Reality, Courage And Self-Esteem

I think this tale has special meaning for adult children raising children. The story of that brave child will most likely fill them with a secret envy.

How many of us would be willing to speak against the collective voice of the adults around us? How many wish we had had that kind of courage as children?

How many of us now would be more like the courtiers than the child, fearful that confronting the emperor's illusions would mean death?

With courage, self-esteem and a link to reality, the healthy child has spiritual independence. His perception and self-expression are not clouded by fears of rejection, abandonment, guilt or shame.

As adult children raising children, we tend to think that such freedom is too risky in the real world, as it was in our childhood home. We keep our thoughts and feelings to ourselves.

Meanwhile when we become parents, we try to put on our own invisible robe of parental authority and wisdom, for which we feel we have paid dearly. We think that it will protect us from all the things we most fear.

Luckily for us, we have children who will confront our illusions and get to our essence, as if all our cover-ups were transparent. Our children speak to our child within, no matter how uncomfortable it makes us. They help us to discover our own spiritual majesty while we are trying to help them discover theirs.

Your Home As Your Castle, And A Little History

I believe that it is no accident that adult children raising children are center stage today. Only two particular situations, of relatively recent origin, can isolate a family so much that an addicted parent can control the family belief systems like an emperor, drawing her or his whole family into co-dependency.

The first situation is that of the detached, suburban development home. The second is the economically mobile, anonymous apartment dwelling.

In more traditional lifestyles, extreme isolation and family anonymity were far less attainable. Community intruded more often. Whether in an extended family situation so characteristic of American cities before World War II, an interdependent farming community, conditions of extreme poverty, or even conditions of extreme riches, one or another elder, youngster, neighbor or servant would be likely to share the nakedness of the emperor with a child and help him or her maintain grounding with reality.

But in isolation, parents can create their own set of rules, double standards, reverse value systems and more, with little chance of the child being exposed to a different view.

We may wonder why modern schools have not offset this isolation. Of course in some cases they have. But the major reaction patterns have already been learned by school age.

In addition, much of our educational system reinforces certain co-dependent illusions, namely . . .

1. Others can rarely be trusted.
2. Competition is the only natural pattern between equals.
3. Hierarchical authority is the only natural pattern between unequals.
4. You cannot be trusted to figure out what you need to learn or when you need to learn it, nor to learn it on your own.
5. Performance is more important than self-expression or excellence.

Today we face the strange phenomenon that we may not even suspect we have a problem because so many around us have it too. We see so little true happiness or health that we start to believe that happiness is merely the absence of pain and that health is simply the absence of disease. We lose our faith in anything higher than ourselves — in our value or our spiritual connectedness to each other.

One of the most tragic problems in the field of addiction in the 20th century is the prevalence of dependency among those we look to as models for happiness and health. Popular myth has it that since famous and wealthy people have everything already, it is only moral weakness if they succumb to addiction. The public blames them morally, all the while imitating their excesses and dependencies.

Luckily, after two, sometimes three generations of addicted or co-dependent families, many celebrities are coming out of the closet with their problems. From Betty Ford to Robin Williams on addiction and from Suzanne Somers to Linda Gray on adult child issues, our society hopefully may be collectively seeking recovery.

For adult children raising children, as for the larger population of people with co-dependent traits, the self-treatment discovered some 50 years ago by the founders of Alcoholics Anonymous is still the most successful program for recovery. Addiction expert Joseph Beasley, M.D., in *Wrong Diagnosis, Wrong Disease*, and philosopher Thomas Powers in *The Great Experiment*, give similar explanations for the success of these groups.

They rely on a triple combination of regular inspirational reading, regular fellowship with others who share their common problems and goals, and regular self-examination with the help of the 12 Steps to Spiritual Enlightenment that were developed by the Oxford Group over a century before.

My fondest hope is that this book will become one of the readings you treasure most in your recovery as parent and person.

Privacy And Anonymity

"We too have been lonely and frustrated," begins the preamble to Al-Anon meetings where families of alcoholics share their efforts to grow out of the problems of co-dependency.

The details of my own story will remain untold in order to protect the privacy of the family and friends of the chemically dependent person who affected my childhood.

Anonymity is a cornerstone of the most successful recovery programs. For people who suffer from addiction and who are considering seeking help, it is comforting to find that they do not have to reveal publicly the nature of their problem in order to get help.

Likewise for the families and friends of chemically dependent people, anonymity helps take the moral sting out of being associated with an alcoholic or other addict. These people are all too aware that our society still tends to find fault or look for blame in families of addicted people. They also fear the repercussions on the addicted person they love.

This is despite the fact that experts are convinced that alcoholism and other chemical addiction is a multi-factorial physical illness that cannot be caused by or blamed on another person. In other words, alcoholics are alcoholics no matter who their parents, spouses, other relatives or friends might be.

In practice, families of addicted people may need to be even more careful about anonymity than recovering addicts themselves. This is because if they reveal their co-dependent identity, listeners may guess at who in the family has the addiction and every member of the family is suddenly suspect. In addition, even if the listeners guess right, only the alcoholic and his doctor have the right to give a diagnosis.

Anonymity serves another crucial purpose as well. It reminds us of our spiritual identity and shared humanity independent of our name, address, money, job, religion, failures or successes.

For these reasons, all cases described in this book including my own have been altered to be unrecognizable. If anyone believes they recognize themselves in these pages, it is because of the

ubiquity of their situation, not because of its uniqueness. Rest
assured that I have not told anyone's story, not even my own.

My Personal Story

Within these bounds of maintaining the anonymity of those I
love, I want to share a few generalities. Although affected by alcoholism, my childhood was rich in many ways and I accept and am
grateful for the love and support of my parents and the camaraderie
of my siblings. Indeed, I feel that if I could have been so deeply
affected even with the "ideal" situation I had, then anybody could
be. And wherever I go I find that they have been.

I have spent my professional life training people about their
rights to self-determination and freedom. First as a lawyer I helped
people assert their legal rights. Then as a health trainer I helped
people assert their rights to health and well-being. When I became
a parent, I sought through my first book *You Can Postpone Anything
But Love* and hundreds of seminars to help others assert their rights
to be good parents.

It was through my parenting experience that I discovered my
adult child issues and my need to assert my right to be myself. It was
through that incredible dedication of a parent that I found the
courage to look again at my own life experiences. It was with a
sense of purpose not to pass on any unnecessary pain that I came
to terms with spiritual reality.

I discovered that roles I had played for years were not always the
real me. As an oldest sibling, for example, I prided myself on my
perfectionism and workaholism.

Schools and other authorities praised these traits. I maintained
them first to please and then to help define who I was. All the while
I felt deep down that I was out of touch with my true self, but I
wasn't even sure it was there, and I postponed the search.

Meeting the challenge of being an adult child raising children
has been one of the most enlightening processes of my life. I began
with a search to find out how to unblock the full expression of my
parental love and continued into a deeper search to discover, para-
phrasing anthropologist Louis Leakey, why I am who I am and who
made me that way.

More than any other search of my life this one has led me to real,
reliable answers.

Using insights from my own case, together with hundreds of
other cases I have known, I want to share with you the rock bottom
common denominator of adult child co-dependency patterns among
parents, so that you can end the cycle of co-dependency for you and
your children now.

Out Of The Parent Trap

Raising children today is a challenge for anyone. It demands
steady commitment, a strong sense of self, flexibility, enthusiasm
and more. For those who were themselves raised in co-dependency,
the challenge can be overwhelming.

Trapped between parents and children, we fear both the old and
the new. Do we follow the old patterns we know didn't work or do
we flounder in the unknown, exhausted and confused?

Either way, will our parenting reflect our inner struggle in ways
that, try as we might, will trap our children into the same co-
dependency?

Perhaps in addition, we have been drawn to mentors, spouses or
lovers who recreated our comfort zone, the familiar though un-
healthful co-dependent patterns. Now, as parents, can we avoid
perpetuating these patterns?

We can. In my thousands of contacts with adult children raising
children over the last six years, I have been struck again and again
by these facts:

1. Adult children are among the most dedicated of parents.
2. Regardless of the nature of the addiction in the childhood
   home, the issues that face the adult child raising children are
   amazingly consistent.
3. These issues derive from the central issue of co-dependency,
   that is, the failure to learn what you can control and what you
   cannot — in the parenting context, the failure to learn that you
   cannot and must not try to control the inner life of your child,
   and that you can and must control your own words and actions.
4. The block in parent-child relations is more often in the
   parent's perceptions, low self-esteem and fears than in any
   aspect of the child.
5. It is surprisingly easy for parents to begin their own recovery
   by finding people who will affirm their personal worth and
   will show them new options and thought processes that will
   give direct experience of personal worth and power for good.

6. The simple, practical tools and options that work to raise healthy children apply equally well to "reparenting" ourselves, in order to unlearn our faulty learning and learn a new way of life.

7. Parenting options are available equally to fathers and mothers. Likewise, options for the child-parent relationship are available equally to our sons and daughters. Parenting skills are person skills, interchangeable between the sexes. Recent studies confirm, for example, that fathers in nurturing lifestyles are as nurturing as mothers cast in that role. Indeed, sexual differences emerge in their full, beautiful distinction to the extent to which artificial differences are not imposed by false assumptions. (In this book, please do not imply any limitation of sex from the choice of pronouns in any particular case. In case histories, they have been chosen primarily to make it easy to distinguish one actor from another.)

Prepare For A Spiritual Adventure

In this book you will discover that all our children really need is for us to be ourselves, our truest selves. Through a compassionate review of your reactions to your childhood experience and a better understanding of how your children restimulate these reactions, you will find out who you really are and how to be that wonderful person for your children.

You will see how certain stages of dependency and co-dependency in your family of origin may have contributed to your personal choices from among the various clusters of reactions — namely rejection, defenses, manipulation and despair — that we can develop in response to an addicted parent.

You will see how these recognizable clusters result from the central tendency of co-dependents — to make our happiness dependent on the behavior of another — and how they become a template for later relationships, including our link with our children.

You will see how these habits of reaction contribute to our parental insecurity and family conflict in the key areas of parenting — affection, performance, authority and trust.

You will grasp useful tools to overcome these habits, whether yours are subtle or sensational, mild or major. You will learn how to reparent yourself in everyday family situations at the same time that you are building your parent-child relationship and becoming more the parent you want to be.

You will find that being good to yourself will inspire you with new ways to be good to your kids. Empathizing with your own inner child will show you how to empathize with your children. Accepting and forgiving your parents' mistakes — and your own — will help you let your children learn well from their own. And trusting the guidance of your own inner vision will show you how to trust your children to be the children you want to love.

You will find within yourself the strength and courage to release the old and to welcome the new.

The ideas in this book are meant to be inclusive rather than exclusive, eclectic rather than dogmatic. Many of the ideas are not new but put together, perhaps, in new ways that can help you gain new insight into yourself and your special challenges in being a parent.

Rather than rules and prescriptions, I seek to give you tools, options, metaphors, perspectives, suggestions. I do not claim to know all the answers. I am comfortable defining an expert as someone who sees things in a bit more depth and breadth than most.

Only you can find the answers for your life. I seek only to persuade you that you have the right, the freedom and the power to find your own answers, to liberate yourself from your past and to energize your life and your family's future in a way that makes you proud.

A Few Pointers

I am convinced that it is possible to live from one moment to the next totally in the present and in continuous direct contact with universal reality and joy.

To paraphrase the theatrical play *You're A Good Man, Charlie Brown,* happiness can be anything, anything that you love. Charlie found a pencil that his idolized girlfriend had chewed and was happy, knowing that she was human like him.

No thing is inherently right or wrong. We establish moral value by how we use things. Whether sex, bulldozer, dagger, stapler, humor, command, medicine, atom, book, fence, words or whatever, it is always within our power to use things for good or evil. Good intentions do not always make the difference. Now is the time to learn how to use our gifts in line with the good within.

We cannot wait for others to change. I discovered my own co-dependency when I was trying to change someone else's co-dependent behavior!

The more we try to change people for the better, the more they stay the same. The more we try to respect them and appreciate them, to love them for their goodness as they are, the quicker they change for the better. The central paradox of relationships, this is true even for our relationship with ourselves.

We must be good to ourselves and learn to value and love ourselves to be able to grow and to help our children grow.

George Bernard Shaw said the quickest way to ruin a man was to destroy his self-esteem. If we have made many mistakes in the past, they do not make us morally culpable in the present unless we use them to keep ourselves down.

With this book you will find that what you thought were mistakes in the past may in fact have served a valid purpose at the time, and that what were real mistakes may have been beyond your power as a child to avoid, or were made with the best knowledge and skills available to you at the time.

Avoid dwelling on who deserves blame for the past and discover how to remove any blocks present now to becoming the parent and person you want to be.

How To Begin

To make a running start on the suggestions in this book, do the following:

1. Decide not to try to do anything differently towards your child for at least a week.
2. Set aside five to ten minutes each morning to anticipate your parenting interactions for the day in light of the ideas in this book.
3. Set aside five to ten minutes each night to review your parenting interactions from the day in light of this book.

Read through this book at whatever pace is comfortable for you. Put into practice any parts that appeal to you and that fit within your comfort zone of acceptable risk in family relations. Then come back to the book again and see if you find more ideas you would like to try.

In this book you will learn how to feel grateful when your children declare openly, even when you least expect it or want it, but often when you most need it, that your protective robe is not really there. You will learn with their help that you don't need any protection from them or yourself. And you will find at last that you don't want it.

By that time you will have found that it has already slipped off.

I hope you will come to view your special challenge as an adult child raising children as a liberation and an exciting adventure that adds to your humanity and the love and joy you share with your child.

Good luck to you!

Your Turn
To Be Parent

2

An eager child stands on the sidelines, waiting to be called into the game. She watches the others having fun, catching the ball, dropping it, praising and blaming each other. She waits for her turn. She practices behind the bench, watches intently, cheers on the others enthusiastically. She serves the juice at break and helps the teacher watch the time. She waits her turn.

It never comes.

For adult children of co-dependency, the feeling that your turn never comes can last a lifetime.

Perhaps when you were a child, it never seemed to be your turn to be carefree, blame-free, innocent, with time on your side. You were asked to be grown up too soon. You were careful, responsible, brave and parsimonious, or you felt guilty about not being so.

Carefree children were in other families, silly, childish, going nowhere. You never got your turn to be just a child.

When you grew to adulthood, you thought it would be your turn to be a confident, authoritative grown-up, to be in control, to do what you wanted, to make the rules, to say no to hurtful behavior, to be happy.

But you may have found yourself tilting at windmills, or afraid to take risks, or overwhelmed with work and ambition, or tormented by a vague emptiness and lack of hope. Bad habits may have crept into your life and you fought them by trying to be more perfect, or by giving up on yourself.

It still was not your turn.

Now you become a parent. At last it is your turn to make the rules, run your own household, have the authority, set the schedule, have the fun. You can insist on a close family, honesty and affection, fun holidays, mutual love and support.

But the chief fun you saw in your parents was often their compulsions. They rarely played with you. You may discover you don't know what to do to have fun as a parent with a kid. You may not know what to do to get close.

And what makes a holiday happy? Parenting may give you none of the satisfaction you hoped for to fill the gaps in your adult life. In fact, your children may remind you of your parents in strange ways. And they seem to ask even more of you.

Your turn still hasn't come. In fact, you may even begin to feel as a parent that you have entirely missed your turn, that it is gone, a mere mirage, and you have only now to grow old and die.

When we see our children growing up before our eyes, we may start to believe the game is over, that we'll never get our turn, that all our efforts will reap no reward, no pleasure, no sense of being alive at all. We may begin to wonder whether parenting was a mistake, whether we will ever grow up ourselves, whether we are adequate parents, whether childhood is meant to be a drag after all.

Cynthia

Cynthia spoke quickly. She adored her children and thought they were as fine as could be. But her frustration was acute.

"I know I do all I can for them but I always feel I don't do enough. I don't play with them as often as they ask. I feel unappreciated when my husband leaves parenting to me, even though he's a good father. I wish I could have them see more of their grandmother. When my father died just before my first was born, I had hoped his birth would somehow have given Dad a reason to pull his life together."

A model child, model daughter, model wife and model mother, she didn't have any idea how to accept that she was good enough for now, that she had done all that was necessary for today, and that she could relax and enjoy life, if even just for a quarter hour.

Low Parental Self-Esteem

I have met hundreds like Cynthia, women and men, who are trying their hardest to be great parents but have left out one key ingredient. They have forgotten to like themselves as parents. They don't know how to take pleasure in it just for its own sake.

Why is it that adult children find it so hard to like themselves, to enjoy themselves, as parents?

As we identified in the first chapter, the special parenting challenge for adult children raising children is the confusion and low self-esteem generated by the conflicting messages from parents and children about our intrinsic self-worth.

It is a conflict many adults have when they become parents, but the child raised with co-dependency struggles with it on a different order of magnitude. It is a spiritual struggle for her very life.

As children we are completely unaware that the injuries done to the family by a chemically dependent person are a result of the mood-altering effects of the chemical. We are completely ignorant that neglect of our emotional needs by other adults in the family is the result of their fear and preoccupation over the behavior of their dependent loved one.

When our needs are not met, then, we must assume that it is because the world is no good, our parents are no good, or we are no good. The first option is out for a young child because the life force is strong and survival is paramount. The world is at least good enough to warrant the instinct to survive.

The second option is out for a young child because survival is impossible for a human baby without the care of loving adults. To reject parents is to give up life.

So it is the third option we settle for.

Then every criticism, every challenge to our competence or motives, every putdown, every addiction-serving complaint, and every mistake or performance short of perfection seems to prove that our low self-esteem and self-blame are correct.

The natural self-esteem with which we were born — that life force, that desire to connect with the universe, that sense of spiritual value just for being you — slowly dies.

We choose from a large selection of survival tools and reaction clusters, as we shall see, to deal with this spiritual deficiency. But we never learn to like ourselves again.

When our children come along, they let us know that our old reactions are obsolete. It is time as adults to look back, to make new choices, to let go of compromises to our self-worth and limits to our growth, to reinterpret old messages, to become author to our own lives, and to take charge of our own destiny.

Our children know that if we gave them birth we are meant to be their parents. They will accept nothing less. We are the universe to them, all warmth, security, inspiration, fun, validation. They have no need to blame us, find fault, sabotage us or put us down. When we think they are doing these things, it is our low self-esteem sabotaging again.

Accustomed to tests, to challenges, to negative expectations, or even to sabotage in our young lives, we are on our guard for signs of failure. We start to see our children as our chief critics, our last judge, our highest court. We feel them watching us, we feel we must never slip.

But as we watch ourselves self-consciously, we are ever more prone to slip. And tensions rise. We develop a hidden agenda, wanting to prove once and for all that we are good and right and have always been so, but we deeply suspect otherwise and want to hide it.

We can't get to like ourselves as parents because we are still looking out only for the bad in ourselves.

Profile Of Adult Children Raising Children

Adult children raising children have a unique profile of special characteristics:

1. They *lack role models* for parenting that they can admire.
2. They have well-developed and often *unrealistic rules* about how they think children should behave.
3. They have a vague but chronic feeling of *uneasiness* about their parenting, rendering them especially vulnerable to criticism, popular theories and self-doubt.
4. They have a *sense of urgency* in their parenting, that they must do everything right, right now, or all will fail totally.
5. They *feel trapped* by duty, to children, spouse, house, parents, work or all of these.
6. They put rest, recreation, laughter and *fun last* on their priority list, and yet work hard to make time for others to relax.
7. They find it hard to express their love, having been conditioned to the chronic *suppression of unconditional love.*
8. They *look outside themselves* to other family members as the source of their happiness, lacking confidence in their own resources and preoccupied with how others, including their children, will view them.

9. They rarely ask for help from others, instead assuming that if something needs doing, they must do it. They have an *exaggerated sense of responsibility* — self-reliance to a fault.
10. They are very clear on what they do not want for their children but have no idea what they want. They motivate themselves and often their children by *disincentives,* having little faith in positive incentives.

These 10 specific traits lead to a typical bundle of feelings in adult children raising children. There is anger, self-pity, rebellion, mourning, all those things a child can feel when her turn never comes.

We can feel abandoned, alone, left out. Overworked and unappreciated. Helpless and out of control. Yet responsible for everything. Angry, even enraged. Bitter and uncaring. Petulant and moody. Depressed and resentful.

Parenting seems to lack a lighter side unless it is a stolen laugh born out of helplessness.

Often we are aware of none of these feelings. We may feel only confused and inadequate. Or angry at others for taking advantage of us. We may decide that it is not worth it to have a turn at life, that what good feelings we do get are at the expense of someone else. We may feel secretive and guilty even when we feel happy.

Our Children As Rescuers

Above all we want to be rescued. We feel unloved, tired and hurt. And a vicious cycle of self-hatred can set in if we catch ourselves expecting to be rescued by our own children.

Our self-worth seems doomed. After all, isn't it folly to hold a fantasy that our children can rescue us, release us from our exaggerated sense of obligation, give us our turn?

We may presume that since our own needs were not met by the parents we loved, children's needs must be endless. We do our darnedest to meet them, to the point of exhaustion and beyond, but ultimately doubt that we have done it or that it can be done.

We don't realize that we are still hanging on to the perfection of our parents and to our imperfection as children, refusing to come to grips with the errors of our parents, to recognize our own helplessness and innocence as children, and to learn to love and forgive our parents and ourselves.

Instead, we expect our love for our child to finally give us the love relationship we always craved, yet we find ourselves estranged the more we insist.

We may fear it's them or us. If we insist on enjoying ourselves, we fear we will deprive them of their childhood all over again. We jump back and forth in roles from rescuer to intimidator to victim, not sure who is what when.

The disappointments of alienation from our child can be the last straw, the lowest blow in our lives. We must heal or die in a spiritual sense. Our words and actions are so powerful, yet we find we have no direct power over the course of the parent-child relationship. We cannot predict or control. We need something to rely on inside us to direct us, because results outside only confuse and mislead us.

In a very real sense we ask our children to parent us, to play the old part again for us so we can get it right this time, to be the parents we didn't get enough of, to make us feel valuable in ways our parents, because of their illness, were unable to do.

We feel we face our last chance to have happiness. But still no one is giving us our turn to have it. How can we pass the test if no one gives us a pad or pencil? Is this the source of those recurrent dreams that we're taking a test we haven't prepared for?

The Oddness Of Being A Parent

When we see our children leading an almost carefree existence, we may feel guilty, jealous, wrong, hopelessly idealistic, over-protective.

Other times we are envious. We want to drop everything and swing from a tree. Or get right down and play with jacks on the floor. We want to run into the wind, forget our jackets on a spring day, laugh in the rain, shoot each other with water pistols, hammer on grandma's piano, jump on the bed.

Sometimes we are so eager, we take over our kids' projects, in the guise of showing them how better to do them, until we realize that this is exactly what was done to us when we were kids, by frustrated parents or teachers.

We may bemoan the lack of time to play. We fill our lives with doing what's right, what's necessary, what's good. Or we punish ourselves, fall into depression, and seek companionship and solace for not doing all these things. Either way we schedule out any real time to enjoy life.

And we find ourselves blaming our children. If we didn't do so much for them, or didn't feel we should do so much, or if they didn't want or need so much, we could "relax" more.

We know it's not up to them to give us our turn, but we sometimes blame them anyhow. We're caught between our parents and our children and have lost ourselves.

Here are some examples of the conflicting messages you may wrestle with:

Messages From Your Parents

1. Children are unreliable, powerless, overdemanding.
2. Children are bad and uncontrollable.
3. Love of children means martyrdom and sacrifice.
4. You are helpless, inadequate or stupid on your own.
5. Life is a difficult, mixed prospect.

Messages From Your Children

1. Children are powerful, simple, innocent.
2. Children seem inclined to be good.
3. Love of children can be fun.
4. You are all-powerful, gifted and awesome.
5. Life is to be happy with.

Reinterpretation, Forgiveness And Letting Go

Once we have our self-esteem on the mend, we can get a grip on reality, take courage and reinterpret the old messages in light of the ring of truth we can now recognize in the new ones.

Old messages can be reinterpreted as follows:

1. We need to accept and forgive others for having made the old messages and interpretations necessary.
2. We must forgive ourselves for keeping them too long.
3. We can forgive ourselves for blaming parents who were unable because of their addiction to form any moral intent at all, much less any desire to hurt us.
4. We must let go of our grip on the old messages, regardless of the many purposes we have used them for in the past.
5. We need to reinterpret and rewrite the old messages according to spiritual principles that put you and your child on the same side.

Once we realize our power over our own lives, we can see that it is entirely up to us to give ourselves our turn. We must lift all self-limitations and believe in our own self-determination. We must telescope our lives, taking all our turns in a matter of a few years instead of decades, so that we can catch up to our kids, and so that we can enjoy being parents before our parenting years are over.

Impossible as this may seem, we soon discover that we can live a lifetime of turns in a moment if, instead of pining after missed opportunities of the past, we get in touch with ourselves and our children on the spiritual level and realize that all of eternity is in the present moment.

This telescoped enjoyment, this rebuilding our sense of self and our power as spiritual beings, this feeling of being whole in ourselves and valuable to others, is the thrill of a lifetime that can begin any time and last a lifetime.

Parental Guilt And The Child As Mirror

In our parenting we need to come to grips with the idea that our children are often a barometer of our relationship with ourselves. It is the best indicator we have, yet we often ignore it because we are so actively avoiding taking on any more guilt.

But it is hard to ignore that when we are depressed, they are cranky. When we overwork ourselves, they are overdemanding. When we are at peace, they are playful.

We are their models for emotional power, self-esteem, personal growth and spiritual self-determination. It has been said that we teach others how to treat us by the way we treat ourselves.

It is inherent in the human species for the child to learn by copying, mimicking, imitating, mirroring the parent. We have the longest growth period of any species on earth precisely because our long apprenticeship to our parents is essential to teach us the intricate technological skills and social patterns that have been responsible for the success of our species.

But this pattern of reflecting the parent does not mean that the parent is meant to control the child's being or can if she wants to. The parent can look to herself and to the way she relates to the child. She cannot focus on changing the child by direct action without asking for disaster.

The spiritual distinction between influencing others positively, on the one hand, and taking responsibility for their lives, on the other hand, is an important one throughout our recovery. We each do what we can on any day, and our children have their own path to follow. If we help them, this was meant to be. If not, or if we have made mistakes in the past, this was also meant to be. If we dwell on what might have been, then we will miss our chance today to be what we can be.

I find it helpful to think of the parent-child relationship as a third entity independent of either parent or child. There is you, there is your child, and there is your relationship — the connection, the link, all that bundle of words, body language, actions and expressions, that teach one about the other and you both about your connectedness. Neither can force the other to change to suit his or her personal goals.

One can surely use physical force on the other to obtain a certain immediate result. But he has no control at all over the consequences, any resulting change in the other, or any effects on the relationship. The only way we can expect good to come from our interaction as parents is if we focus attention not on the child and not even on ourselves alone but on the way we interact with each other.

Sparing The Pain

With parenting we want so much to do it right, to pass on the benefit of our experience, to spare our children from pain.

But it is a paradox of life that we cannot save another from pain. We can only help them learn how to use it. We cannot predict where someone else's pain will come from but we can set an example of what to do about it.

Our surest way to save them pain is to set an example by trying to truly feel our pain, to accept it, to value it, to move through it, to forgive any and all who we have blamed for it, and to move into joy.

Pain that is denied is passed on. Wrongs to ourselves that we have not mourned and let go become the "sins" of the parents that are visited on the children, try as we might to prevent it.

Our children will not avoid the pain we suffered by overprotection, by careful orchestration of lessons, by a martyred parent, or by the close-to-perfect parent.

They will avoid it by being loved unconditionally by a parent who models self-love, who accepts joy and play from within, who communicates with feelings and about them, who radiates and resonates with a willingness to increase her self-knowledge and self-determination in life with her child, and who looks to her spiritual self, not her child, to heal her pain.

The special challenge of the adult child raising children is to find herself. To learn to ask for her turn and to believe that this is it, if she is but willing.

The spiritual energy of your children demands that you rethink your image of children, of yourself as a child, of your parents, and of yourself as a parent. You must find yourself as a person and learn to love that person in order to be the parent you want to be.

When you do this, your turn will have come, long awaited, welcome, none too soon, but exactly on time, in plenty of time.

Parents' Catch 22: Is Your Child Being Affected?

3

The more adult children raising children try to avoid the mistakes of their parents, the more they tend to repeat them.

This is the Catch 22 of co-dependent parenting. You determine what parenting behaviors you will not duplicate from your childhood, and then you set your mind to avoid them. You fail to realize that it is the determination and the setting of the mind to avoid that are the real traps, not the particular behaviors.

Our private compulsion to be unlike our parents can be as preoccupying to us as dependency or co-dependency was to them.

This Catch 22 does not mean that we are powerless to change or to improve on the pattern we were given. The key to understanding this strange mechanism is to distinguish between two different levels of the parent-child interaction, the behavioral and the spiritual.

Shopping List Of Unwanted Behaviors

The parental behaviors that adult children seek most to avoid when they become parents can be summarized as follows:

1. Inconsistency.
2. Excessive, irrational or arbitrary rules.
3. Distance, lack of warmth and affection.
4. Preoccupation, lack of good listening.
5. Misinformation, lack of information.

Instead, they plan to be consistent, rational, affectionate, attentive and honest.

Most adult children expect that these goals can be accomplished by hard work, lots of talk and introspection, being available and expressing love frequently.

Dedicated as they are, however, two things happen. First, they find these new behaviors harder to do than they expected because they lack any model or experience. The plan comes from their rational mind. In an emotional situation it is hard to stick to. Flip-flopping back and forth, they have already lost on the consistency point.

Second, the particular behaviors they tend to choose in these broad behavior categories may be as misguided as the ones they are trying to avoid. Unless they realize that the ones they are avoiding arose from a whole range of possibilities in face of a serious illness of the spirit, they will not recognize that the alternates may be equally co-dependent.

The problems on the spiritual level, then, can make it impossible to achieve healthy patterns at the behavioral level, regardless of our intent.

Sally

Sally's husband was the son of alcoholic parents. She was acutely aware of the denial, lack of communication, lack of warmth and maddening inconsistency that she saw in her husband's family. She felt that her husband had little knowledge of how to be warm, communicative or empowering to his children.

She was patient with him, knowing his struggle. She did her best to give lots of warmth, guidance and time herself to her children to help overcome the paternal lack.

What she found was that her children were "taking after him." They were reluctant to share or to receive affection, had periods of painful rebellion, denied any emotional pain, and were not enjoying the happy carefree childhood she so wanted to give them.

Forgetting Ourselves

Sally had identified all the behaviors she wanted to avoid or change. She was going about it as best she knew how, with great dedication. What she didn't realize was that her strategy needed to have her at the center, not her children, not her husband, nor her analysis of her husband's family. She had not addressed the spiritual level of her relationship with her children in the context of co-dependency.

Sally knew that her parents had had a co-dependent relationship. But she felt she had dealt with her mother's alcoholism long ago and knew how to lead her own life and be a loving person.

But when she began raising her children, she did not realize that her parents' parenting strategies were still her own on the spiritual level.

Many adult children who are recovering have been surprised to discover, sometimes by talking to a parent, that their parents had the same hopes and plans that they do now — to be consistent, rational, affectionate, attentive and honest.

Most of us have a string of promises of things we will do and will not do, just the opposite of our parents. But what we don't realize is that our parents were well-intentioned too.

Until we accept that they had an irresistible impediment to healthful parenting, we will not accept that, try as we might to end the destructive parenting behavior, we can fall victim to the same ineffective strategies because of a spiritual gap which we have inherited.

Bad Spiritual Habits Passed On
In Parental Co-dependency

The spiritual habits that were the real source of parenting strategies in the adult child's childhood home can be summarized this way:

1. **Other-centeredness.** The addicted parent was centered on his or her chosen chemical and the strange effects of his or her relationship to it. The co-dependent parent was focused on the addicted parent's behavior, or on the children to protect them from the results of the other's behavior, or both.

2. **Willingness to hide the truth.** The parents tried to protect the children from the effects of the compulsive disease in the family. Misinformation and inconsistency were therefore inevitable. Denial was a way of life.

3. **Low self-esteem.** The inability to do anything about the addiction of another and the constant pain inflicted by the other's behavior on those close convinced the parents of their inadequacy. They devalued their parental power to love and guide as well as their basic personal value, and likely

resorted to innumerable rules and cold absolutes to direct
their children's lives.

4. **Negative world view.** With so much discomfort and no knowledge of how to end it, the parents adopted a pessimistic view
of themselves, children and the world. Distrust and self-doubt
lead to inconsistency and a suppressed capacity to love.

These mistakes of the spirit in an addicted or co-dependent household are the real burden of inheritance for the adult child raising
children, until you consciously put down the burden. The parenting
behaviors that troubled you as a child and led to your list of resolves
is only the tip of the iceberg of spiritual pain.

Sins Of The Fathers (And Mothers)

An old adage says that those who don't know history are condemned to repeat it. We think that if we analyze what our parents
did wrong, we can avoid repeating their mistakes.

But no matter how much we want to be consistent, rational,
affectionate, attentive and honest, we will fail if we just change
behaviors without changing the spiritual attitude.

If, like Sally, we determine to put at the center of our lives
protecting our children from the truth of our troubles, the other-
centeredness is still there. If we hide, deny, belittle or cover up
someone else's behavior or the effects of our own childhood experience, willingness to hide is still there. If we minimize our own
powerful parental influence for good in our children's lives, then the
low self-esteem is still there. If we perpetuate a sense of helplessness, the negative world view is still there.

In Sally's case she thought she had made dramatic changes. In
reaction to her mother's neglect of her, she was not only attentive but
making up for her husband. But in both cases her children absorbed
the message that the father was at the center of the mother's life —
the same message Sally absorbed as a child.

Likewise, by trying to alter the children's impressions of their
father, she was perpetuating the willingness to hide, just when she
thought she was showing her husband's truest nature to them.

The patterns of co-dependency are inherited in ignorance and
struggle. We are not condemned to repeat them. The sins of the
fathers are not visited on the sons without our spiritual complicity.

No matter how impressive are the statistics that these co-dependent patterns run in families, we are entitled to live free of them.

Because of the power of the mind, of parental love and of the human spirit, we can stop this progression of "inheritance," even in one lifetime — our own.

And we can start by understanding our parents' travail. We can start by letting go of the idea that they sinned at all. Through the explosion of scientific and investigative examination of alcoholism and chemical dependency in the last few decades, we now know that these dependencies are more akin to the disease model than to what we think of as crime or sin.

I think the model that best explains the incredible burden on adult children raising children is inheritance of the same spiritual illness that the addicted parent had as part of the threefold illness of addiction — mental, physical and spiritual, as they say in Alcoholics Anonymous. It is the spiritual gap, the lack of faith in the goodness of ourselves, our children and the universe, that leaves us open to repeat the mistakes of our parents.

With this model, the solution is evident. We must stop struggling on the level of particular parental behaviors. We must stop letting our preoccupation with imperfections increase our other-centeredness, our willingness to hide, and our loss of faith in self and in the world. Instead we must fill our spiritual gap. We must work on this deeper, or higher, level and seek our solutions there.

In Sally's case, she worked to accept who her husband was just as he was, along with his bundle of inherited behaviors. She let up on protectiveness and oppressive over-concern about her children. She focused on her own set of adult child reactions to revise them in light of her present understanding. The struggle against all the old behaviors became unnecessary. And her children responded each step of the way.

Increasing Consciousness

The assumption that we will be like our parents has merit if at all, only for unconscious living — the things we do out of mere habit. We are free at any time to consciously change virtually any behaviors that are accessible to our conscious decision-making.

But even habitual behaviors we can pull into consciousness and change, if only we believe we can.

In *The Origin Of Consciousness In The Breakdown Of The Bicameral Mind*, psychologist Julian Jaynes states that over 80% of our lives are lived unconsciously. No wonder we see family resemblances in our behavior!

But this is not inevitable. Jaynes postulates, as have many others, that the spiritual evolution of man has but barely begun. When we become conscious of our spiritual connection to each other and the universe, we have a complete 360 degree range of choices at any given moment and no one can predict that we will behave in any particular way or like anyone else. We can live consciously most of the time, if we wish.

How To Recognize The Spiritual Gap In Parent Or Child

If chronic self-doubt and morbid determination haunt us in our parenting behavior, and it may stem from a spiritual malaise, is there a way to recognize the spiritual gap directly?

In order to develop the motivation and courage to begin change in our family life, it can be helpful to discover what signs, if any, of spiritual malaise there may be in our family relationships.

It is easy to dismiss the need to change, after all, when the parenting choices we wrestle with are not uncommon and may not, we might reason, be related to our adult child issues.

But you had best avoid such complacency. In all likelihood your child is being affected if you come from co-dependency and if either you or your child is showing any of the indicia described below.

Some Signs Of Sickness Of Heart

1. **Chronic failure of communication.** Either you or your child does not talk at all or feels frequently misunderstood or misquoted by the other.
2. **Guilt over broken promises.** Either you or your child feels that commitments aren't kept often enough to each other or to yourselves, or unrealistic promises are being made.
3. **Emotional isolation.** Either you or your child fails to share emotions with the other or selects which emotions to express. Typically we tell our children how they *should* feel in different situations, and we share our own feelings only when we have sifted them down severely until we think we are feeling what we think we *should* feel.
4. **Excessive demands.** Either you or your child feels over-worked or underappreciated, making excessive demands on yourselves or each other and feeling responsible for the

health, happiness, security or contentment of each other,
other people or the world.

5. **Suppression of unconditional love.** Either you or your child
resists easygoing signs of affection, like touching, choosing to
be together, sharing thoughts, interests or events. Typically,
the child asks why if you suggest doing something together,
and you find yourself analyzing whether the child will accept
or suspect a gesture of affection, or whether he deserves or
has earned a hug, a release from chores, a gift, an extra phone
call and so on.

6. **Bundle of negative feelings.** Either you or your child expresses
a sequence of feelings that goes something like this: "Whatever I do is crucial to the survival of everyone else, including
me. I'm too tired, incapable, old, young, unattractive, cowardly,
stupid, etc., to do it all. No one else cares."

7. **Suspicion.** Either you or your child spends a good deal of your
time together giving or demanding explanations and reasons for
things. You may second-guess the child's responses to outside
events and words, and fear the worst. The child may get un-
usually agitated or sullen when plans fail or routines are upset.

All these signs can be experienced by either you, your child or
both. Often we watch for signs in our children, ignoring ourselves,
and breathe a sigh of relief when we don't notice anything. But if we
feel uncomfortable, our children are being affected whether we see
it or not. If we don't pay attention to ourselves, we may just not
know what to look for.

Or we may pity ourselves for our pain and fail to notice effects on
our children. We may even blame our pain on what is going on in
our children without realizing which is cause and which is effect.

With spiritual matters, if either parent or child is feeling down, the
other will reflect it, either by a mature, spiritually affirming response
or by an equally powerful negative reaction.

For sure, these signs can arise in any family and will from time to
time. But if in looking over this list the frequency of these events in
your family bothers you, chances are your adult child traits are
affecting your parenting. It is time to find out which key areas are
most affected, the subject of the next chapter.

Key Sensitivity Areas For Parents 4

To discover what core beliefs we have adopted from our family of origin that may be sabotaging our efforts to be the parents we want to be, we need to identify the areas where we are most vulnerable to the control of the co-dependency cycle. It is there that we must begin to replace our outmoded beliefs and behaviors, one at a time, with more realistic, courageous and self-affirming attitudes and actions.

The four areas in which we are most sensitive to having our old patterns restimulated are the areas of touching and affection, performance and mistake, teaching and authority, and trust and maturity.

You may notice that they correspond roughly to developmental focuses in the child's life, from infancy to preschool to school age and then to puberty. But all areas have their sensitive moments throughout a child's life.

Marion

Marion felt unable to get close to her preteen son. When she touched him, he recoiled as if approached by an undesirable classmate. She was at a loss how to get through. Saying, "I love you," as she did every night, got no response and didn't feel like enough.

She bemoaned that she did so much for him, made his breakfast, prepared his lunch, found excellent tutors to help him in English, went to all his soccer games, yet felt no satisfaction as a parent.

31

Her mother had been an alcoholic and hadn't been there for her. She thought that if only she had been closer to her mother, there might have been something she could have done. She had deep guilt over this. Now she was doing for her son all she wished her mother had done and still she was not close to him.

Touching And Affection

If touching and affection are a sensitive area for you as a parent, you may be caught in this conflict: You want to be loving toward your child but you find it difficult to show overt affection without fear of appearing inconsistent or overindulgent.

You may also simply lack confidence in the process of expressing love and receiving it. You may lack a model for unconditional love. You know you yourself crave lighthearted gestures of affection but you harbor a sneaking suspicion they must be earned or paid for later. You rationalize that overt affection may spoil the child if it is not tied to the child's being good.

You may fear that if you are too generous with affection, it will not be available as an incentive to good behavior. You probably don't believe that virtue is its own reward because it never felt particularly good to you when you were virtuous — that is, you did what you were supposed to do — as a child.

Besides, you're just not sure how to do it. You don't want others to raise eyebrows about possible incestuous overtones or even to kid about it when they see a lot of touching. Nor do you want to flatter your child into an unrealistic egotistical picture of himself that may be shattered by future friends.

You may even feel jealous that no one shows you spontaneous, overt affection. You feel afraid for the child. You don't know what it would be like to grow up that way. At least you know that one can survive growing up the other way because you did it. Is it worth the risk to try something different?

Instead of simple touch and affection, then, your parental love might take the form of overindulgence with toys, lessons, material advantages. Or it may take the form of excessive worry.

You may find it almost impossible to say "I love you." You may hear old tapes that repel you, like, "I am only doing this because I love you." Or "You know I love you, that's why . . . . " You may distrust the very words.

You may associate love with control, thinking that wanting the best for someone and doing all you can to get it for them is love. But love is not wanting and doing. It is seeing and enjoying.

To love a child, you simply find the good in your child and you celebrate it. To love you need not lift a finger or knit a brow. Love is not an emptiness — a desire to be filled. Instead it is a fullness, an outpouring, ready to be shared.

Touching and affection can be sensitive issues at any time during your lives together. Typically the most obvious times are morning and night, hellos and goodbyes, anniversaries and holidays, personal successes and failures, times of joy and sorrow.

But the solutions come in the in-between times, when the loving atmosphere you want can be most easily cultivated. Our garden needs both the rain and the sun, but we do our best gardening in between, on a cool morning or a cloudy afternoon.

The times of tension in this key sensitivity area of parenting can become times of opportunity for healing, as we will see in the chapter "From Rejection To Affection."

Bev And Sheila

Bev was eager to have her daughter Sheila succeed. She put in extra time with her as the teachers urged, to help her overcome her low performance in numbers. She helped her every night, going over the lesson beforehand with her, reviewing for any errors and patiently helping her correct them.

Teachers saw the effort being made but Sheila's performance got no better. Teacher and parent began to suspect learning disability.

Bev was an adult child who had worked herself extra hard in school to get the good report cards that helped, she had thought, to keep her out of the limelight of family troubles and complaints. It hurt her greatly to see Sheila having trouble performing to the teacher's expectations.

Performance And Mistakes

If performance and mistakes cause anxiety to you as a parent, your mixed messages are probably these: You want your child to set his own standards and find his own motivation but you tend to be a perfectionist and take responsibility for the behavior and progress of your child.

We are programmed as parents to empathize with the activities, experiences, mistakes and triumphs of our children. Our reaction is important for validating and guiding their young lives. We help give them the social feedback that prepares them for adulthood.

In this sensitivity area we need to look very carefully at our own motives. Their performances no doubt can reflect our success in a positive way — making us proud of the training we have been able to give them as a result of our economic success, the drive we've given them as a result of our own laudable ambition and the confidence we have instilled as a result of being good parents.

But watching and enjoying must be distinguished from controlling, second-guessing, expecting and counting on our child's performance.

If we get our love of our child mixed up with his or her performance in any particular activity, we broadcast dangerous mixed messages.

So often we actually teach our children to take mistakes and failures harder than they would naturally merely by assuming that they will take them hard because we did as children. We may be oversolicitous and comfort them excessively, so that they come to believe that mistakes are a sign of inadequacy or that, at the very least, we parents tend to exaggerate things.

I have been surprised how easily well-validated children accept mistakes and move on without any negative impact on their next try.

We may have to completely rewrite our personal encyclopedia of success, failure, performance, mistake, doing, being, risks and security. At the least our motives in responding to our children's experience will need serious examination.

In a workshop one time I found that out of seven mothers, four had distinct recollections of being severely embarrassed during a performance and receiving no empathy or appreciation for their feelings.

Performance Anxiety

Becky had completely forgotten her lines in a school play. Her mother assured her that no one noticed.

Mary had had her wig fall to one side and heard the audience giggle. Her mother had told her she had done a wonderful job and Mary said nothing about how she felt, thinking that she had better just try to enjoy the praise.

Alice had lost a race, performing way under her personal best. Her mother had said, "Don't worry, I know you can do better. I'm sure you will next time," and continued chatting with her friends.

Joyce had addressed all her Valentine cards with the last name first instead of last and had been laughed at when the cards were passed out in school. Her mother told her, "It's nothing. Don't be so sensitive. Your friends don't know anything."

All of these women had taken major life lessons from these early experiences to the effect that their feelings didn't matter and that perfection was to be expected and mistakes hidden.

They now had to rethink these conclusions as they raised their own children.

This sensitivity area includes many milestones of early childhood, from toilet-training to tying a shoelace, from first words to saying please and thank you.

It also affects later experiences, including learning to ride a bike or drive a car, school days, sports and competition, questions of manners and social interactions, making friends and getting along with relatives.

We will explore the power of our parental expectations over our children's performance capabilities in the chapter "From Defenses To Self-Expression."

Susan

Susan was very upset. She gave her children more freedom than she had ever had as a child, and still they did not respect her the few times she did assert her authority. She tried to be very clear when authority was to be obeyed, like visiting at others' homes, when out in public, when at school or in dangerous situations like climbing in mountain parks.

But the children were rebellious daredevils and seemed to have no respect at all for parent or teacher.

She remembered being a cut-up herself at school but thought that it had been a rebellion against repression at home. Now she tried to run an easygoing household and she still had rebellion on her hands.

Teaching And Authority

The inner conflict in the key area of teaching and authority usually shows up this way: You want to be patient and understanding, but it

is hard for you to tolerate challenges to your authority when you
believe you know best.

This key area permeates almost all parent-child interactions where
the parent has an agenda for the child. Sometimes this is all the time,
every minute of the child's life.

I have heard innumerable parents say they could never teach their
child and are thankful to have them in school. This is primarily a
result of their own experiences of being taught in a classroom
setting all their lives and consequently associating learning only
with hierarchical authority. We have no conscious model for learning
in a cooperative, interactive, experimental and creative way.

If you assume that teaching occurs only when one person has
authority over the body and mind of the other, then being a parent
is bound to challenge you in this key area.

It is the lack of a role model of parent as mentor, sponsor, guide
and inspiration that makes teaching and authority such an issue
for adult children raising children. Certainly ultimate authority
must rest with the parent. But if it is resorted to in any situation
that is less than a once-in-a-blue-moon emergency, it is likely to
communicate parental distrust of the child and make the child
less likely to learn.

As a matter of fact, we are always teaching as parents. The stim-
ulation of life exposure, the necessity of invention towards real-
life goals and teaching by example are the true models of teaching,
rather than the stiff, *memorize-what-I-tell-you* model of conven-
tional schools.

If we can identify some area where the child has learned successfully when we didn't really know we were teaching, such as in
smiling, talking, using a spoon, speaking on the phone, hugging
and so forth, we can use that as our model for rewriting our rules
about parental teaching and authority.

It is at our weakest moments that we fear threats to our authority
and insist on symbolic acknowledgment of it. Our children know
this. We have already lost when we think we have fallen back on this
ultimate weapon.

We may win the battle, the battle of wills, but we have lost the
war, the war between love and fear. Extracting due respect for
authority is just one of the many futile manipulative tools we may
use to hide from ourselves our essential powerlessness to alter the
way our children feel and act by force of our will.

Aesop's fable in which the wind could not force the coat off a
man's back but the sun by its warmth inspired him to remove it, is

a perfect model for parental teaching and authority, as we shall see in the chapter "From Manipulation To Communication."

Angela

Angela was afraid to trust her preteen to sit for the baby. He seemed gentle enough, but he was so easily distracted by life that she feared that almost anything could happen.

Her father had been an alcoholic and her mother worked to make ends meet, so she had often been left to care for her smaller siblings. In fact she had always felt that she was like a second mother to them.

She found it impossible to believe that her own son would now be capable of that same kind of responsibility. Yet she knew other mothers' sons sat regularly and she did not want to deny that she had successfully raised a loving, caring child.

Trust And Maturity

Learning to let go of your children is a continuous process beginning at their birth. The mixed messages in this key area of trust and maturity occur this way: You want your children to trust you and to develop maturity, but you tend to be so busy yourself proving your own trustworthiness that you never take time to gain confidence in the growing maturity of your child.

You fill your precious child-oriented time with "what ifs" — what if he gets with the wrong crowd, what if he forgets to turn on the headlights, what if his first girlfriend breaks his heart, what if he climbs up too high, what if his father forgets to pick him up and on and on.

You feel you must still earn the trust of your children and others by excessive work and by taking on extra responsibility. You want to trust your children, but you have so overloaded yourself with duties that you do not give yourself enough time around them to see just how capable they are.

And many of the duties you have taken on are ones that they could do and should do, to give them the opportunity to demonstrate their growing maturity, to themselves and to you.

To take one common example, you may resent when they are late but find yourself making excuses for your own tardiness because of taking on more than you can handle.

While you are busy tending to the child's imagined needs, you are fearful to ask the child about his or her needs, since you believe from your own experience that children's needs are insatiable. Otherwise your parents could have met yours.

Or you may believe that children don't know their needs, because your parents repeatedly told you that you did not know yours.

As happens so often, a few denials to maintain your childhood belief system lead to faulty logic, and one bad conclusion leads to another until you are reacting to completely illusionary assumptions.

With you otherwise occupied and not taking the time to delegate appropriately, your children may be taking on less of the responsibilities they could handle and more of the ones they are not ready for. Latchkey children are a prime example. You may feel guilty about this uneven delegation, but instead of discovering other options, you may wallow in worries about whether they can handle all they try to do.

Then you may blame yourself for holding them back with your fears and you may increase your sense of urgency, because they seem to be growing up before you have had your chance to give them what you want.

They respond to your self-imposed pressure by taking it on as a way of life, either by mimicking it or rebelling. Either way you feel uncomfortable and even more unequal to the task of parenting, managing your household and all your other roles.

The mixed messages about trust and maturity arise most often in the context of choosing friends, scheduling homework, setting priorities for time and recreation (TV and video), selecting activities and hobbies, exploring sexual feelings and intimacy, taking risks and setting goals in sports, work and lifestyle. More examples will be explored in the chapter "From Despair To Trust."

Snow White's Stepmother As Adult Child

The wicked queen who tortured Snow White's youth gives a very unbecoming but illuminating portrait of the adult child raising children in the extreme of co-dependency.

This lady could tolerate nothing at all from the child she so much wanted to be like. She was supersensitive in all areas, having settled on competition and jealousy as her only emotions toward the child. She ignored any relationship with the child, did not know how to enjoy her and, in fact, set about to destroy her.

The woman wanted to be beautiful and she stared into her mirror by the hour, seeking outside approval and acknowledgment of her beauty. I used to wonder why the queen didn't stop looking in the mirror if the mirror didn't tell her what she wanted to hear. But she was caught in the vicious cycle of low self-esteem. She lacked the self-validation mechanism that comes with adult maturity.

The child Snow White was a constant reminder to her of her imperfection. The more she knew of her, the more approval she craved and the more she distrusted her flatterers. The more she tried to hide her hideousness from herself by destroying the child, the more hideous she became with trickery, disguise, dishonesty and treachery.

Futilely she thought that by changing Snow White (killing her, fairy-tale style), she could persuade her flatterers and herself that she was okay. But it was only when her mirror was destroyed entirely that her wickedness and ugliness were destroyed (killing her also, fairy-tale style).

Her ugliness ended only when the whole idea was abandoned that a reflection was needed to prove her beauty. As long as she was caught up in seeking outside approval to counteract her low self-esteem, she had no power to love, only to destroy.

It is interesting that Snow White had her own co-dependent behaviors. Her self-esteem too was low. She only found personal value in mothering the seven dwarfs and in being idealized and rescued by a prince. She had no idea of her beauty, and she was protected time and again by well-meaning helpers from the sad negativity of the wicked queen.

It is a shame that fairy tales so often painted the co-dependency syndrome so well but never gave us a clue as children how to heal it. On the contrary, we were encouraged to behave like its childlike victims and wait to be rescued.

Of course most adult children as mothers will not become wicked witches but many have feared it from time to time.

Competing With Your Child

Is it possible that in all these key areas we are competing child to child?

We find it hard to give affection because we are still trying to get it. Our child's level of performance makes us uneasy because we don't know yet if we have ever performed satisfactorily. We don't trust the natural lines of authority because we are still trying to discover if we have any at all. We can't count on the child's natural maturing process because we haven't had it yet ourselves.

Illusions Of Love

With all these mixed messages and resulting fears, doubts and rationalizations, we stay hypersensitive in our key interaction areas. Try as we might to love our children, we keep turning up with strange illusions of it. These may include:

- Protection, financial support into adulthood, worry, inquisitiveness, sacrifice and lectures, instead of affection.
- High standards, earned praise, "constructive" criticism, multiple expectations and sympathy, instead of appreciation of excellent performance, validation of effort and acceptance and empathy for mistakes.
- Commands, ridicule, tests, pressure, rules and lessons, instead of creative play, self-directed learning and authority based on inspiration and meaningful example.
- Overprotection, projected doubts and fears, warnings and rescues, instead of trust and increasing responsibility with increasing maturity.

Now is our opportunity to let go of these illusions of love and fill our days with real love — love of ourselves as well as of our children.

In the next chapter we will take a closer look at our childhood programming for parenthood and how to reprogram it, before we go on to the specific patterns of reaction that need to be overcome in our dealings with our children.

Where You Got Your Parenting Program 5

The starting point for adult children raising children is the model of their own parents. Whether they embrace it or run the other way, it is the chief influence on their parenting style until they make a conscious change in their parental attitudes.

In their childhood home, co-dependent children develop a kind of learning disability that prevents healthy growth by trial and error, reality testing and positive reinforcement mechanisms.

This blockage to normal growth leads to distorted interpretations of their perceptions and cumulative misinterpretations that lead, in turn, to ever more numerous energy-sapping habits and inappropriate reactions.

Until these are consciously changed, the co-dependent parenting style continues in a host of diverse disguises.

As adult children raising children, we often decide to do all within our power to avoid the same pain for our children that we experienced. But we are likely to create similar conditions for them to the ones we knew, albeit by different means, unless we find new models, reactivate our learning, reinterpret old experiences, and review all our habits and reactions with an eye to weeding out the bad and building on the good. The key to our old misinterpretations lies in feeling our feelings.

Our ambivalence as adult children raising children comes from the resurrecting of old mixed messages that we thought we had put to rest. In our childhood, we had dual sources of information that were in intolerably frequent contradiction.

We heard conflicting explanations from different relatives trying to fabricate excuses for inexcusable behavior.

We heard messages of blame either directly or indirectly from our relatives that conflicted with our innate sense of our own limited responsibility for others and our own unlimited spiritual worth. Often we had different messages from home and from other sources, especially school.

Now as parents, we get messages from our children that conflict with the compromise interpretations we have developed from those earlier contradictions.

Noticing how we feel in response to our children is the leadline to finding our old faulty programming and letting go of habits that serve us no longer, once we let go of our underlying need.

A Faulty Model

The first thing to go in the life of a chemically dependent person is their love and trust of others. They can't love others if they can't love themselves. With an addictive chemical at the center of their lives, the expectations of love within the family only remind the addict of his pain and serve as ready targets for the defenses and manipulations that go with the mood-altering nature of chemical addiction.

It should be no surprise that adult children raising children have little familiarity with the many possible options for manifesting unconditional parental love in any or all of the key sensitivity areas. They cannot recall examples of everyday gestures of affection, appreciation of effort, enjoyment of product, forgiveness for mistakes, child-led learning, reasonable authority, intrafamily trust and acceptance of change and maturation.

Even if you did experience these from some adults in your life, maybe a teacher, an aunt, grandfather or friend, you may have little idea of how to mix these with the everyday stresses and responsibilities of being a parent.

Often we think our parental models were not so bad so long as we survived, and especially if we did not suffer dramatic abuse like being beaten, sexually abused, neglected physically or abandoned by our parent. But the subtleties of parenting and negative messages that you absorb even from small incidents can lead to big effects many years later in your own new family.

Learning Disability

Learning is a special province of the human child. The tutorial relationship she or he has with a parent is absolutely critical to survival in our highly social, behaviorally sophisticated and culturally dependent species.

In a healthy family we learn quickly, by gaining the approval and delight of our parents when we behave well, and by earning their displeasure and instruction when we behave badly.

But in the co-dependent family there are few if any positive reinforcements.

When the parent cannot give love and validation, there is no positive reinforcement by which to test our learning. Survival is the only payoff no matter what we do, with avoidance of pain or guilt being our only motivation to action.

If we always fear the worst, we are always alert to prevent it and almost any behavior which precedes a time of relative peace is automatically reinforced. At the extreme we can develop elaborate routines and lines of thinking that are completely divorced from reality, much like a witch doctor's elaborate chants to prevent lightning.

We become like the primitive tribe that sacrifices lambs to ward off earthquake but never knows when to stop the sacrifices so long as no earthquake comes.

Without a model of other options or a hint of positive reinforcement for a different response, we do the same things again and again hoping for improvement. We become the classic example of total learning disability: We do the same thing again and again expecting different results.

We cannot distinguish which behaviors are effective and which are not. For example, if a parent asked us to do something distasteful, we might whine, swear, yell, sulk or get sick. If we were not forced to do it after all, any or all of these behaviors would be reinforced. Only if the parent were to tell us persuasively why it was their thinking changed independent of our behavior might we alter our plan for next time.

The predominance of negative rather than positive reinforcement in the school environment and later in our working environment only serves to perpetuate this learning disability.

By a very early age we may not even recognize positive reinforcement any more when it comes from other sources or even from a recovering parent. We have learned to suspect affectionate overtures, unconditional praise, increased responsibility or greater freedom as traps, flattery or unwanted emotional debt.

Even a trained mouse in a Skinner maze can do better. But adult children are like the poor mouse whose training maze is rigged with equal shocks throughout the maze. He has no clues at all as to why he gets shocked and why he gets fed. He just runs because that is his nature, until he is exhausted.

We too keep running until we're exhausted.

This learning disability is the primary source of the cumulative misinterpretations of parent, child and life that adult children bring to parenting. It is essential that we quickly reactivate the learning processes through reintroducing positive reinforcement into our lives.

Misinterpretation

As children we learn from induction, from the small to the large, from the hands-on experience to the generalization. Most later learning and almost all formal learning is by deduction, from generalizations — laws, principles, theories and rules — to specifics — people, places, things, feelings and events.

Many experts believe that induction is the kind of learning that makes things stick best in our memories, that makes lessons and messages become truly part of our lives — the tools we rely on in a pinch. And this is the kind of learning we do most of as children.

If childhood experiences are distorted by family addiction or co-dependency, we are likely to have come up with erroneous generalizations about ourselves, our parents and life. If we take these generalizations as the basis for later deductive learning, we pile one bad interpretation on top of another.

We eventually reach a point where our erroneous interpretations are completely dysfunctional. Writer Wayne Dyer calls these our erroneous zones. Our old interpretations of things no longer serve as any kind of guide to reality and we feel without any direction at all.

Parenting is the last straw for many. In my experience, there are at least four times every day that your emotions reach a critical point where you must choose between old and new in your responses to life with a child.

The essence of children is their immediacy. They do not wait. They do not accept excuses, they do not believe lies, they will not stand for neglect of their feelings or essential needs.

If their survival needs are not met, of course, they will learn to wait, to listen to denials, to hide their feelings and so forth. But they will also learn to keep others waiting, to give excuses, to lie to themselves or others and to neglect others' feelings and needs.

When your children "become your parents" in these strange ways, pressing the same old buttons, pulling the same old strings, you have a direct clash between your parent and your child. A cycle of escalating emotions and co-dependent fears is likely to ensue.

Sandra

Sandra felt terrible guilt when her little daughter looked into her eyes with awe and love. She secretly feared that she could never be worthy of that kind of admiration from such a perfect little being. But then a day later, the child would be screaming, "I hate you! You never do what I want!" Ghosts of her helpless co-dependent mother's words of 30 years ago swam in her head and she felt like dying.

Though, like most adult children, she had a well-prepared agenda of things not to do as a parent, she fell back on the old ways. It's hard to be inventive and take emotional risks in the heat of the moment. It was easier to scream, sulk, throw things, say a putdown, get a headache, be sarcastic, develop excessive sympathy or whatever was the old model.

Habits are too persistent to rely on spontaneity in parenting. Then the old tapes are even more likely to play unabated. What we must do is contact our feelings as the leadline to our old interpretations and deal with these in our personal time.

Impostor Feelings

Many adult children have severe impostor feelings, as described in Pauline Rose Clance's book, *The Impostor Phenomenon.*

They feel that they or their families are impostors, that their family wasn't or isn't quite real, that they are just going through the motions, that disaster might strike any time to disturb their superficial peace, that the rest of the world, including their own children, can only be fooled for a limited time into thinking that all is well.

These are very natural tapes for an adult child. Crises could emerge from the least threatening of events, and did in the child's eyes. Situations that seemed fine often turned ugly. He learned to be suspicious of anything pretending to be simple, pure or excellent.

Dana And Trask

Dana was scared when she discovered that her son Trask told lies, even when he didn't have to. Her father had been a master at stretching the truth to explain away his addiction, but Trask had never been exposed to that kind of behavior. She had seen to that. Could it be inherited, she wondered?

When she explored the fears that arose in response to her discovery of the lying behavior, she came to see that she herself was almost pathologically honest, to the point of boring her family with long explanations of her motives and open introspections on her feelings.

She also tortured herself over social white lies and was a policeman of honesty in family relationships, particularly between herself and her husband. She began to see that though lying behavior had never been modeled in her home of choice, the compulsive attitude of suspicion she had projected unknowingly was nurturing a fascination with lying and a sense of low self-expectation in Trask, so that lying seemed to Trask to be a reasonable and interesting option.

Feelings As A Key To Our Misinterpretations

When our child's behavior bothers us, or our relationship is not what it should be, we need first of all to examine our own feelings as a key to our underlying negative interpretations.

Most often feelings of anger, fear, pain, self-doubt, self-pity, resentment and rage are just below the surface. They are the emotions we think we either never felt as children or have long ago overcome.

Anger is the aggressive feeling we get when we cannot control something we want to control. Feelings are not bad or good by themselves. Like other things, it is all in how we use them. Anger tells us that we need to re-evaluate the power we think we have over others. As children we did not know enough to be able to do that. We stuffed our anger deep inside instead, because the people around us made us think anger was wrong and dangerous. It's anger that you were not allowed to express as a child that becomes unexpressed rage as an adult.

By the rules most adult children set for themselves, you are not allowed to express anger to your children now either. In fact often any parental outburst will be vehemently justified by blame on the child or another, which blame must then be validated by the other's apology. We make anger into a much more complex thing than the simple emotion that it is.

After we tune into the emotions our children stimulate in us, we can then find out where they come from. Many of us suppose that our thoughts follow our emotions, emotions being our deeper level of mental activity, at the supposed pre-human level of the brain. But as rebirthing trainer Phil Laut and others have explained, most of the emotions we deal with are the result, not the cause, of our thoughts.

Visceral reactions they are. But they are a response to our perceptions of reality as interpreted through our thoughts. They are not a direct response to reality. Rarely are we faced with the unambiguous fear of a caveman surprised by a saber-toothed tiger. Our fears are more subtle, largely created by our prior interpretations.

When we hide from our feelings, we are protecting ourselves from re-examining old misinterpretations. When we listen to an emotion, feel it and find out where it comes from, we can correct our old misinterpretation. Then we can actually say good-bye for good to the resulting negative emotion.

In this process we may be disappointed to find out that we rarely can rely on a friend to help us decide if our emotions are appropriate or merely the result of old misinterpretations. Rules about when we should take offense, when we should be embarrassed, when we should fight back, when we should rescue or help, all these can be seriously distorted society-wide, at least at the level of popular perception.

So if some aspect of your family life bothers you and the emotions you feel make you uncomfortable, pursue your healing process, even if your neighbor, sister, mother, secretary or pediatrician tells you it is perfectly normal, natural, unavoidable or all in your head. It may be normal but it may not be natural or healthy — it may be learned co-dependency. And it may be healed.

Rage And Forgiveness

We may wonder what doing away with Dana's rage at Trask's lying will do to help Trask get over his penchant for lying. But here is the miracle of parent recovery.

Dana began to allow herself to feel her rage at her father's dishonesty with her, innocent child that she was. She recalled times when he would try to disillusion her of any models or heroes by catching them in some harmless untruth.

Rather than stuff any more guilt about her rage at a sick man, which she knew intuitively was wrong even as a child, she came to accept that a force beyond her or his control, namely his addiction, was responsible. She learned to forgive him. And she learned to forgive herself for her rage, knowing that she was too young when it developed to realize the nature of his illness.

She stopped assuming that without scrupulous oversight and accounting in her family, honesty would be lost and everyone's life would fall apart. Trask's attitudes began to relax as she stopped being everybody's conscience. Lying no longer offered a special challenge, an attention-getting form of rebellion, or a dramatic interlude. More healthy options began to hold more appeal.

The Reprogramming Process

Through this process Dana has:

1. Identified her immediate feeling: She felt rage at having a child tell lies.
2. Found the underlying, terrifying thought it came from: Her father didn't love her and trust her enough to be honest with her.
3. Investigated how this thought was in error by applying her knowledge as an adult: Her father's lying was a result of his dependency and implied no messages at all about his love or intent towards her.
4. Revised her childhood conclusion to comport with reality: Pathological honesty is not a virtue or necessity. Lying is an option that children tend to reject in a healthy, open, supportive environment where parents deal candidly with feelings.

Put more generally, to overcome prior misinterpretations we can follow this procedure:

1. Feel all feelings without judging them.
2. Contact your associated childhood memories about any inter-action that caused similar feelings.
3. Imagine yourself talking candidly to your parents about each memory.
4. Imagine yourself talking candidly with your child about your feelings and memories.
5. Let the memories and feelings rest lightly and find their rightful place in the framework of your reinterpreted experience.

This simple exercise can have dramatic effects on your happiness as a parent.

Letting Go Of Habit

In his book *The Child Under Six*, famous pediatrician James Hymes wrote that the bad habits of our children will eventually disappear when the underlying need is met and that we can assume there is such a need if there is a bad habit. Also if we don't know the underlying need, we can trust the child to tell us one way or another, if we create a nurturing atmosphere.

So too for ourselves, our underlying need must be discovered and met if we want to rid ourselves of bad habits of the spirit that sabotage our parenting.

As adult children raising children, our central underlying need is to understand why it was that our parents rejected us. In recovery we find out that it was not us, nor was it them, it was a crippling physical and mind-altering dependency.

We can develop healthy models for ourselves by hanging around with people who offer them. We can find positive reinforcement in good readings, self-appreciation and regular thoughtful interaction with our children and supportive adults to reactivate our learning ability.

And we can develop from the ruins of our old outmoded interpretations of reality new healthier spiritual attitudes that will allow new perceptions to reflect universal reality.

When you realize the full impact of your parental loss, it seems overwhelming to try to overcome all the habits of life that may be related. Understanding which stage of co-dependency had the greatest impact on you can help you identify your personal set of reactive habits, so that you can weed them out selectively and accurately, leaving intact the hidden strengths on which you can build your new conscious parenting behavior.

Stages Of Co-dependency In Your Childhood Home | 6

Many parental reactions can be labeled co-dependent. With their tendency to fear the worst, adult children raising children can often torment themselves by imagining that no matter which way they go, bad consequences threaten.

The fear of the unknown can immobilize them into complacency and discourage change.

In order to make it easier to identify which reactions are most likely to cause you trouble in your parenting, it is useful to categorize the most common reactions.

The four categories we will use here are rejection, defenses, manipulation and despair.

The preoccupation of the addicted parent with his dependency, together with his willingness to hide and his low opinion of himself and the world, and the preoccupation of the other adults in the family with the addicted parent's behavior, create a chronic atmosphere of rejection, urgency, emotional strain, hollowness and spiritual isolation.

Within this atmosphere the co-dependent family goes through four distinct stages dominated by the addiction. *In the first stage,* the chemically dependent person denies any problem and is relatively functional with his disease.

In the second stage, he can no longer hide the existence of a problem but finds excuses and rationalizations for it, including generous projection of guilt and blame.

51

In the third stage, his addiction becomes disabling to himself and to normal family function.

In the fourth stage, the addict is largely nonfunctional and non-responsive.

Somewhere between the first and sixth birthday, a child absorbs the bulk of his learning about relationships of love and trust. The particular stage of dependency and co-dependency his family is in at that time has a major influence on the patterns of reaction that impress most strongly on him for future relationships.

Like a person who might don a down jacket when stationed in Alaska and then keep it on when he goes south, thinking it is a part of him, the reaction patterns stay with us until we consciously let them go. The zipper that keeps them firmly in place is the low self-esteem, guilt and fear of abandonment at the heart of the adult child syndrome.

Each child tends to feel trapped, rejected, caught in the middle, her turn skipped over. With the learning disability described in the last chapter, the particular pattern imprints powerfully on her mind and becomes a habit. She is essentially arrested in her maturation beyond this point, stuck in a repetitive cluster of reactions.

These stages and the patterns of feeling and behavior that they entail largely determine our reactions today in the key sensitivity areas for parents until we reeducate ourselves.

If we identify which stage of co-dependency dominates our reactions as a parent, we will have an easier time finding and uprooting the negative habits of thought and action that trouble us.

Parenting styles that we tend to view as reflections of basic personality can be discarded as mere reflections of the learned attitudes and behaviors of the co-dependent child we once were.

We can retrieve our basic personality from under the debris and experience healing within our parenting relationship, no matter what role we have assumed in our adaptation to co-dependency. For example:

You can heal that wounded child who can make you into a whining, victimized parent against your will.

You can banish that perfectionist, people-pleasing child who can turn you into a judgmental, impossible-to-please parent.

You can dispense for good with that manipulating, deal-making child who can turn you into an arbitrary, authoritarian parent.

You can renew that desperate, alienated child who can make you into an overindulgent or neglectful, unreliable parent you swore you would never be.

All of these patterns have in common a single source. You, as a child, were cared for by people who would have loved you with all their hearts but for an intervening disease that took the heart out of their love but left only the trappings.

Being a child, you could not leave, assert your right to emotional support and unconditional love, ignore your parents or make changes by legal or forceful action. None of these options was available.

The classic fight or flight response to danger is out of the question also in the case of an emotionally abandoned child. Neither offense nor escape is possible or desirable or smart for a child. There is no way to externalize the pain and stress.

Instead he does the best he can with the incredible adaptive mechanisms of the human spirit. He tries to love his parents. He denies along with them that there is a problem. He defends when they blame it on him. He bargains to get his survival needs met. He threatens to give up when he finds no love in his life.

And then the moment comes for which our human adaptive powers preserve us. The moment comes when he realizes that he can be free. That all his suppressed emotions can be expressed, including his love of self and parents. That his innate trust in life has not been ultimately betrayed as he had thought. He heals and finds spiritual health through recovery.

We will consider now these four stages of co-dependency as they affect us as adult children raising children.

Ellen, Barbara, Magda, Kitty and Ada — Five Variations On The Bedtime Brawl

When faced with similar parent-child issues, different parents will react differently, depending on which stage of co-dependency they settled into as children.

Ellen, Barbara, Magda, Kitty and Ada all had difficulty getting their children to go to bed.

Ellen felt rejected, unappreciated and a failure. She couldn't believe this was happening to her after all she tried to do right for the baby. She stayed with the child many evenings, insisting on good behavior that never came. She found opportunities to have her husband take over the problem, denying that it bothered her or even that it was a problem for her.

Barbara was angered by the problem. She screamed, yelled orders, arranged to be out at bedtime so that the issue wouldn't arise, became defensive when her husband suggested she try something new and took refuge in books that said it was a normal time for family tension. She often blamed her husband, her other children or pets for keeping the child excited.

Magda was convinced she could handle it. She searched for reasons or excuses, including fear of the dark, nutrition, not enough attention and negative influence of peers. She tried bargaining, promising to let the child stay up later another day, offering special events and rewards and asserting parental authority and rules.

Kitty reacted to her unruly child with little emotion. She quickly decided it was no use to try and she let the child stay up until all hours. When he was too tired, she snapped, "What do you expect? You'll learn or you'll die of exhaustion." She took a laissez-faire attitude that bordered on neglect. She felt she had enough to deal with without worrying about this.

Ada went on alert when her daughter wouldn't go to bed on time. She took it as a sign that something might be amiss in her child's life or their interactions before bed. She noticed her personal concern about getting enough rest and realized that she was regularly modeling worry about too little sleep and yet staying up herself. She had lost faith in her own internal clock and had no faith in her child's either. She decided to run some experiments she planned together with her child, to find out how much sleep they were comfortable with. Both recovered from the bedtime fetish.

Each of these women reacted in a perfectly normal common way to an ordinary challenge of family life. The differences correspond to the stages of their childhood environment that had the greatest impact on their interactive patterns.

The Stage Of Rejection

The child of addiction feels rejection when she first perceives that her addicted parent or co-dependent parent is unable to give her undivided attention.

During this stage, the addicted parent has crossed the invisible line that separates an overuser from an abuser. Addiction supervenes and takes control of the parent's life, making it impossible for the parent to express healthy parental love.

In an effort to hide the loss of control from himself and others, the addicted parent blames others for his discomfort, escapist behavior and chemical excess. He draws the rest of the family into accepting his dumped guilt and denying any fault in him.

The child's natural response is to . . .

1. Insist on attention.
2. Deny any problem in order to maintain a sense of personal security based on faith in the parents.
3. Assume guilt for failing to get attention.
4. Feel lonely, isolated, emotionally abandoned.
5. Suffer lowered self-esteem and sense of value.

Children are totally dependent for physical survival on parents and programmed to value their support, interest and attention above all. Yelling and crying are the chief mechanisms from the beginning to get the attention of a parent. In this first stage it is the preferred response. Later, injury or illness may be a more advanced version of this insistence on attention.

In a healthy parent, crying creates an irresistible impulse to help the child and meet his need. For the addicted parent, the child's pain resonates with her own and creates feelings of blame and self-blame, making the parent helpless rather than helpful.

As it becomes clear that needs are going unmet, the child continues to deny any problem with the parents and blames himself for not being good enough, insistent enough, loud, beautiful, smart, cute or needy enough.

For adult children raising children, the rejection reactions show up most in the area of touch and affection. We find it hard to show affection when it was not given to us when we needed it. We may find it hard too to believe that a child would want our affection, when our own parents didn't want it. We may be unable to believe how much affection a child really wants and needs, unaware as we are of how much was denied us in our time.

In our denial of actual rejection, our fear of rejection looms large and we are afraid to take the risk of reaching out to our child. She too can reject us.

We may even blame the child for not being more affectionate with us — "He never did let me hug him, even as a baby" — and the cycle comes full circle.

The Stage Of Defenses

A child born a little later in the progression of the family dependency problem may be more likely to find his comfort zone in the defenses stage as the addicted parent moves down his path of decline.

The adverse effects of chemical excess become irrefutable to family members, even though they may not yet realize or acknowledge the cause. Withdrawal from reality by the addicted parent occurs both at the biochemical level of actual perception and at the level of emotion.

The child begins to hear his parent describe reality entirely differently from the way the child saw it, heard it or felt it. He gets increasingly blamed, overtly or by default, as a contributing cause of family problems.

Anger is a major response. You feel bound to keep the parent consistent with his articulated promises, devotions and duties. You are sickened by hypocrisy and broken promises. You develop a multitude of defenses to deny any guilt or wrongdoing. You try to win approval despite the parental preoccupation and other-centeredness.

You are driven to please the parent, whatever they ask, to try to make sense of unreasonable demands, to force rational behavior whenever possible and to defend against attacks and irrational behavior towards yourself or others.

With friends you may act as if nothing is wrong, expressing anger over slights but making excuses for them at the same time.

For adult children raising children, the stage of defenses has its greatest impact in the area of performance and mistakes. All of life starts looking like a performance. You become preoccupied with what your parent will think of your words and actions and how they might use them against you. Mistakes become intolerable to you because they put you in the limelight, and any mistakes further justify your declining sense of self-esteem.

As a parent, performance from your children seems essential, perhaps the most important thing in their lives. Just being has little credibility or attraction for you and you tend always to be watching your child, or even noticing who may be watching you watch your child.

Just as you took personally the success of your parents' performances and the disastrous consequences of their mistakes, you take personally the performances and mistakes of your children, as a reflection on you or as unacceptable risk to them.

A people-pleaser and a perfectionist, you set high standards for your children and are quick with judgments, criticisms and instruction.

The Manipulation Stage

For the child who arrives at the time when parental addiction has moved into overt dysfunction, the most typical reaction is to decide to force or trick the parents into meeting basic survival needs. Especially in the adolescent years, when new needs are pressing, the child puts less effort into defenses aimed at winning the parents' praise and approval or at keeping them consistent, and more effort into manipulation.

In this stage you feel confident that you know how to "handle" your parents, to "twist them around your little finger," to "treat them like children," to trick them into giving you what you think you need, to bargain with them and to "leave emotion out of it." You are a cool, together person to your friends and you hope, yourself.

In this stage, your addicted parent has settled into the long, descending road. The manipulative games become predictable, from scathing criticism and name-calling to regret and sentimentality, from protests to promises.

Both play the game of expectations, always holding against the other that this or that unexpressed expectation was not met, and accumulating an impossible burden of unanswerable emotional debt on both sides.

In this stage, you tend to decide you don't need your parents, and you find other outside standards to help prove you are an okay person. You are demanding and authoritative.

You are sure of yourself, always in control, confused only in your quietest moments. At those moments you begin to notice that the one who is most in control is perhaps the one most controlled by others. Self-pity grows.

For adult children raising children stuck in this stage, manipulation becomes more and more the only tool, like the spinach that jumps into Popeye's hand at a moment's notice under stress of any kind. You value compromise and negotiation above everything in interpersonal relations and tend to treat your child as a baby lawyer or entrepreneur.

Kids are a match for you. They are sharp. When they manipulate back, bargain with authority or pit one rule against another to justify their wants, you turn authoritarian and offer arbitrary rules that have legitimacy only in your own mind. Endless rationalizations by you and your child become the content of parent-child interactions.

Battles for control quickly become the focus of any conflict no matter how small the original disagreement.

Manipulative skills affect most the key sensitivity area of teaching and authority. We ridicule ignorance or stupidity and command respect and obedience.

We may use these tactics successfully outside the home, but the same strategies that work well at work or club feel unfair and unloving with our children. Self-esteem sinks further, if there is any left.

The Stage Of Despair

When the parents can no longer meet basic needs, the child reacts with despair. If the addicted parent in your life was partly or wholly nonfunctional at work or home during your early life, it is likely that you will be in this stage.

The defenses and manipulative games don't play anymore, because the addicted parent is too sick to participate. The co-dependent parent may continue to play, however, at least for a while.

You don't have any power or control. You don't even know the rules anymore. You come to resent all the conflicting messages you've heard over the years. Shattered expectations and promises haunt you. The old low self-esteem you hid so well in the defense and manipulation stages comes back to overwhelm you.

Depression and despair become paramount. Neglect of self, not only emotionally but now also physically and socially, becomes a habit. You find it hard to put trust in anyone, to bargain or to negotiate anything. Sickness of heart takes over.

You may reject your parents entirely, give up on them, call them names, hate them, feel enraged by them, to the point of having heart palpitations at the thought of spending a day with them.

You lack goals and you may assume a very hedonistic view of life. You feel free of guilt but also free of any contentment or joy.

As an older child you might move out, run away or start some self-destructive habit. As a younger child, the latter may be your only release from despair if you do not find help.

The addictive environment having always been there, neither parents, others nor even experts are quick to grasp that the addiction is nevertheless the prime suspect in the onset of chronic despair in the child.

For the adult child raising children, overindulgence, neglect or abuse are the styles of parenting you may fall into if you are caught in the despair stage. When you feel emotion, it tends to explode out at whomever is near, usually a child who can't fight back. You try not to feel, and the suppression makes the explosions all the more unpredictable and devastating.

The desperate feeling of having no control and no spiritual value will most affect your parenting in the key sensitivity area of trust and maturity.

If you feel untrustworthy and distrustful of others, how can you develop a relationship of trust with your child? And if you are bitter about growing up, see no purpose to it and view life as a vale of tears, is it any wonder that you will suspect your child is not ready for it? Won't their leaving be the final abandonment you have feared your whole life?

Your child may be the only thing over which you have any sem-blance of control. He or she may be the only thing left that makes you feel alive and valuable after all. It is no wonder that you hate to let them go.

It is often that spark of unmitigated love and energy in a child that gives a person in the depths of despair a glimmer of hope for a way out.

The Recovery Stage

Recovery is the stage in which we move out of habitual reactions into conscious parenting. It takes an act of will, but can start with a very small move for help.

In this stage you begin to realize that you cannot live with the constant struggle to get love, nor can you live without love. You quit assuming that there is no love, that it's not meant for you, or that there are only momentary or induced love feelings. You begin to believe that there might be a love of the spirit that comes from the heart unconditionally and that you might be able to tap into.

In the desperation engendered by a painful impasse in your family relationships, you may reach out for help without knowing of or expecting any real solutions.

If we are lucky, we will come in contact with someone who has themselves moved into this stage and can help give us the courage to believe we can have a better life. The anonymous 12-Step self-help fellowships have institutionalized this shared recovery process and are a ready resource for parents seeking recovery.

In recovery we learn to accept without resentment that we cannot get all the love we need from a sick parent or an ailing family. We find love within us and in the irreducible bond of family whether or not we have an opportunity to acknowledge it in ideal ways. We find love too in the larger family of humanity.

We begin to let love in by learning to love ourselves, to reparent ourselves, to make decisions that feel good to us, to ask others for help when we're sick at heart, to believe that we are deserving and lovable and powerful — no matter who we are, where we've been or how much rejection we've suffered.

For adult children now raising their own, despair may seem a more comfortable niche than trying for help or recovery. It is comfortably familiar because of the desperation and crises that may have ruled our childhood home. It may be scary to try something new and nebulous like believing in ourselves when we've got the always present concrete issues of parenting to face and old tools at our fingertips that worked well enough.

But if we allow ourselves to associate with others going through the same personal recovery, we can nurture our faith that we will be better off in our parenting if we take the risk and make the effort for recovery.

Mourning The Emotional Absence Of The Parent

It is interesting to notice that the five stages described by Elisabeth Kübler-Ross as essential to the process of mourning bear a rough correspondence to the stages of co-dependency described here. The stages of mourning are denial, anger, bargaining, depression and renewal through acceptance.

We are in fact going through a kind of mourning process, as we learn to accept that our parents cannot fill our needs for parental love and support no matter what we do.

We might think that a child born into an addictive family would not mourn the loss of something he never had. But we were programmed as human beings to expect a nurturing parent-child relationship. When it doesn't come, the pain is real, just as hunger for a child born into famine is real.

One of the most tragic things about the child of addiction is that to all outside appearances there has been no loss. The parent is very much there. But the emotional abandonment the child inevitably feels with an other-centered parent is real. If we focus on the mourning aspects of the stages of co-dependency, we can describe them as follows.

In the stage of rejection, you deny the alienation of your parent, take on personal blame for the loss or find other excuses for your parent's failure to meet your needs. You will deny that anything is wrong, expecting things to change or that you'll wake up and find things better.

In order to protect yourself from panic and abandonment, you deny to yourself that your parent is not there for you.

In the stage of defenses, you feel anger. You try to set things right by insisting on fairness, promises met, signs of remorse. If you are young enough, rather than rebel in anger, you may internalize your anger and develop various unrecognized neuroses and compulsions that rationalize your predicament.

As you move into the manipulation stage, you cool off a bit and, cultivating a cynical attitude, you feel capable of surviving anyhow, by your wits. To deal with the loss you search for ways to compensate, like substitute parent or authority figures, material wealth or comfort to fill in the emotional gap or emotional manipulation of the parent to get your needs met. In this stage you believe you can control or manage the loss by minimizing it and bargaining spiritual values you no longer believe in for more immediate needs.

When these tactics fail, the full pain of the loss confronts you. In the stage of despair, your will to live is threatened, just as in the classic mourning stage of depression. Often we do not know where our depression and malaise come from. We may fantasize that our loved ones, even our children, would do just as well without us.

Kübler-Ross sees the early stages as a natural defense mechanism that allows us to avoid the full impact of a loss until we are ready for it. If we have been allowed to move through each stage, we are eventually ready for the last stage of the mourning process, the acceptance stage, when the loss is actually healed.

In the recovery stage we come to accept that the pain we have felt was caused by the loss or absence of the kind of parent-child interaction that a human baby is entitled to expect. And we come to accept that the loss was not meant to hurt us but was the unkind result of a serious disease.

When we have completed the mourning process we emerge with the ability to go forward, renewed in our faith in ourselves, others and the essential goodness of the universe.

Kübler-Ross believes that most of the psychological problems with loss and death come from getting stuck in one or another of these stages.

This is what happens regularly to children raised in co-dependency — so much so, that we have considered the stages of co-dependency as a sequential process only for the adults in the childhood family, not for the children. Because of their youth, ignorance and limited experience, they rarely move from one stage to the next. They get stuck permanently in the stage of greatest impact in their early life until they consciously seek a way out.

Your Sibling Birth Order 7

I once heard a speaker describe a skit she had witnessed about a co-dependent family. (The term was not used yet at that time, however.) She described characteristics in the various siblings that sounded all too familiar.

For the first time I had to ask myself whether traits by which I defined myself were a part of me or were learned adaptations to the past.

So many characteristics we think are inherent in our personalities are only reactions we learned early that had survival value attached to them in our subconscious by the fact that we did survive. These natural but erroneous associations need to be disassociated if we want to find the source of our parenting problems.

Sarah

Sarah was extremely frustrated over her daughter, who was rebellious, had no sense of responsibility by her standards, appeared thoughtless, was undedicated at school and had little moral sense.

Her older son was a model child, and her second son had been okay too. She wondered where she went wrong with this one. Sarah had always prided herself on being conscientious, honest, true to her word, thoughtful, dedicated.

What she found as she explored recovery, was that she did not like herself as she was, any more than she liked her daughter. She always wished she were happy-go-lucky, more able to be playful and carefree.

As she explored her own childhood, she discovered that as the oldest daughter she had taken on extra emotional responsibility for peace in the family and with it a sense of guilt for failure in this impossible task.

With a vague sense of her own low value, reinforced by frequent discounting of her emotional needs by her parents, she took refuge in seeing herself as the embodiment of the qualities her parents had expressed the greatest admiration for.

She cultivated reliability and dedication, even though she didn't really like herself that way and had a nagging sense that it was a coward's way out, that life was passing her by, that she was not the center of her own life. She centered her attention on others' needs, and when she had children, they became the other-focus at the center of her life.

She gradually realized that she had her own agenda for proving her self-worth, independent of her relationship with her present family. Her secret agenda to prove her value as a parent by over-dedication was almost as disastrous in her new family as was her father's secret agenda to find an excuse for starting the cocktail hour early in her old family.

Her child was getting the same feelings of rejection and excessive demands that she had had as a child, only not being the first-born, she chose reactions that tended to be very different.

Her sons may have also reacted typically for their birth order but without her noticing because they were boys. As is common with adult children raising children, she was inclined to identify more closely with the child of her same sex, resulting in an intensification of the co-dependency issues.

The conflict between what Sarah thought she wanted and what she really admired in her child was like a mirror to the conflict within herself. When she learned to set aside her first-born daughter defenses, her daughter soon toned down her dramatic contrast.

They came to a better understanding of each other through a better liking of themselves.

The Co-dependent Family Portrait

In the skit described to me, the first-born was the "little mother" of the family (regardless of sex). A superchild in every way, she got good grades, did what she was told, helped out the younger ones and never told a lie.

The second felt second best. Seeing the older child's life as boring and too demanding, she sought dramatic ways to get attention. She resented the older one's apparent perfection and stretched the truth with fantasy or fluff to avoid always being the subject of parental criticism, negative comparisons and complaints.

The third was the clown of the family. She shrugged at the blame that always tended to land ultimately on her shoulders, or she tried to laugh it off. Never taken entirely seriously, she enjoyed relative freedom from parental pressure, playing the part of the already lost soul.

If there is a fourth child, she may choose one of these three or a combination. She will cover up, protect and make excuses to the outside world for the extremes of behavior in the family.

These adopted personalities have various labels, but we can use these taken from Joseph Beasley's *Wrong Diagnosis, Wrong Treatment:* the **compensator**, the **opportunist**, the **scapegoat** and the **enabler**.

Since hearing this story, I have seen again and again in group sessions, parenting workshops and counseling, how these patterns can predominate over any other predispositions of personality, inheritance, models or experience.

Is it any wonder that we don't feel comfortable with ourselves, when we are in fact not ourselves?

As these siblings grow up, they may choose work, lifestyles and mates that match their chosen pattern but do not suit their basic self. The uneasiness continues.

In this co-dependent family portrait, the dependent parent's addiction is at the center of family life, without family members knowing it. The children often perceive the co-dependent parent as the greater problem because he or she has assumed responsibility for the whole family.

The dependent parent has drawn the other parent into a well-intentioned but destructive co-dependency role and they both attempt to hide, deny and justify the inevitable distortions in family life. To the children, they form a united front that isolates the children from any help in coping, much less any healthy parental interaction.

Meanwhile, the co-dependent parent has also assumed the chore of protecting the dependent parent as much as possible from the consequences of his behavior, a role that has been aptly labelled "enabling." Neither the cause of, nor responsible for his behavior, she nevertheless enables him, by her protective behavior, to continue his addiction with a minimum of adverse consequences. She may successfully control the information and reactions of employer, clients, friends and so forth, but she cannot control or prevent the emotional consequences to the children.

Each child assumes roles and develops strategies not only in response to the progressive distancing from the dependent parent but also in response to the co-dependent parent's multiple enabling strategies and to the evolving clusters of reactions of all other siblings.

The effects of sibling birth order serve then to modify and complicate the child's primary reactions to the stages of co-dependency as outlined in the previous chapter.

While it is impossible to predict which role any specific child will choose, the most frequent sequence of sibling roles can be identified.

Compensator

If you are the first-born, you are most likely to have the weight of the world on your shoulders and to drive those around you crazy with your heavy demands on yourself and on others. You will quickly be identified as a supermom, superdad or workaholic.

You may expect your children to be perfect or appear to be perfect. You will most likely be disappointed that one or all of your children can't, and don't even want to, meet your standards.

As the first-born, you are most likely to have known your parents before their addiction was at its worst. You may have had a bigger taste than your siblings of what consistent parental attention and understanding can be. You may well have become stuck in the stage of rejection, where the increasing effects of addiction, together with the gradual withdrawal of parental attention, was too much to bear and denial became a way of life.

If something went wrong, you developed a program that would say, "It's not that bad. It wasn't really like that. I can fix it. I'll just try harder and it will be all right."

With siblings you may champion the parents, making excuses for their behavior, minimizing the pain or justifying the complaints. Meanwhile you try to get the parents to live up to their dreams and promises.

With your children, you persist in trying to create and emulate an ideal family and ideal world. You become a cruise director and orchestra conductor for your family and feel unappreciated for your efforts.

Opportunist

If you are the second-born, you may be mystified by the Camelot sort of vision of your older sibling. You let them take all the praise for academic achievement and try to pick some area completely different where you can excel and get attention without competing. You may achieve at sports at all costs, for example, ignoring injuries or accidents.

You may unconsciously take on hypochondriacal symptoms to get parental attention. You may lie to get the freedom you need, denying guilt or wrongdoing just as neurotically as your older sibling takes them on.

As you emerge into adulthood, you may be drawn to work that allows for dramatic flourishes, heroic deeds, attention-getting events. You pride yourself on courage and ingenuity, fight for freedom at all costs. You are highly competitive behind a noncompetitive self-image.

You may feel that once out from under your parents and older sibling, you want to be more responsible, no longer "second best," but in the struggle you rarely feel good about yourself.

As a parent, you tend toward perfectionism. You will not tolerate the tactics you yourself once used because you always felt they were a cop-out. You insist on pathological honesty in your household and are overprotective, fearful that your child might take the same risks that you did.

Still you may feel torn because these gave you some of your own most meaningful memories of fun, adventure, being your own person and receiving parental attention.

Usually by the time this second child came along, the parents could no longer hide their abnormal behavior from themselves or their children and began looking for excuses for their failures. The failure of the second child to meet the high standards set by the firstborn overachiever is a ready excuse, much to the detriment of the second child's peace of mind.

As the second-born, you were most likely caught in the stage of defenses, when you develop strategies to try to force or win back the love of your parents. You may alternate between strong-arm tactics and wild efforts to please.

Threats of severed relations alternate with report cards of how you have followed instructions. Where the oldest sibling meets disappointments with her everpresent guilt, the second feels overpowering anger.

Like the first-born, you never feel at ease with yourself, knowing intuitively that you are every bit as capable as the first-born. No matter how much you admire your own daring, attention to duty and efforts to meet impossible challenges, you long for simple acceptance as you are.

Your children will admire your daring and assertiveness but will be challenged by your hidden agenda to be top banana at last. They will most likely choose reactions different from yours, at least initially.

Scapegoat

As the third or last born, the baby of the family, a child learns quickly how to stay out of the thick of cross-fire by making everyone laugh. You know how to break the tension, be the center of attention for a time. You act as a scapegoat or distraction from the increasing malfunction of the family unit. You may never have known any kind of consistency in parental attention or emotional support, and there-fore, you put no conscious value on these.

As you emerged into adulthood, you may well have continued to play the lighthearted throw-away in school, in friendship groups and in work situations. A pleasure to have around, you are popular and the envy of your older siblings.

But the feelings of being misunderstood, unappreciated, perhaps an impostor under your cheerful facade and not being taken seriously when you need it, nags at your self-esteem.

As the third child, you were most likely stuck in the stage of manipulation. You get what you want by devices of distraction, humor, contriteness, apologies and more. Belittling basic emotional needs, you get by.

As a parent, you are dedicated and serious about parenting, often torn between keeping up your nonchalant image and wanting to get serious and really do things right at last.

You might find that your children do not take you any more seriously than your parents did. Or they may react to a perceived double standard when they learn how playful and outrageous you were as a child and yet must still deal with the standards you try to enforce now within your new family.

You may still tend to laugh off problems, try to ignore them, or take center stage to defuse the tension.

Some may perceive you as too emotional, when you feel that your feelings are never really heard or understood.

Whatever you choose in a given situation, you will tend to feel your power is limited and keep your ultimate expectations low since you are accustomed to being low man on the totem pole, last one for the hand-me-downs.

Enabler

A later child will tend to mimic one of the others or the co-dependent parent. You will tend to be a rescuer and a peacemaker, sometimes a manipulator as well.

Jealousies

Each sibling perceives themselves last for different reasons, the first because she puts her needs last and never even asks they be met, the second because she feels the first got all the attention and the third because she is never taken seriously.

In addition, each resents the next older for leaving the childhood home first and leaving them alone to cope.

This breeds serious jealousies among siblings as they grow up. Many adult children watch enviously at other pairs of siblings who are pals, call on each other for acceptance or help, and move roughly parallel through life, sharing their ups and downs. Yet with their own siblings there is constant strife, sudden resurrection of old jealousies, closely guarded secrets and manipulative tensions.

This loss of siblings can be altogether as devastating to adult children as loss of parental attention, especially when what emotional consistency and support was experienced in childhood may have come largely from either an older or younger sister or brother.

Fortunately when either of the sibling pair begins to find what is really her and what are roles and rules she assumed as part of her survival strategy in her childhood, it is possible to begin to mend the tear between siblings.

It is very hard going though, when one has begun to face the family issues and another is still struggling with her habitual survival strategies.

As a result of these sibling problems, adult children raising children lack not only the natural support of their parents, but also the familial ties of their sisters and brothers, who would be aunts and uncles to their children and the parents of their cousins.

Breaches between siblings that result in estrangement of cousins are unbelievably common among adult children raising children and add to the sources of confusion in the children's lives.

Another interesting thing about sibling order is that regardless of where you fit in your family of origin, your parenting pattern tends to reproduce the same atmosphere as the one you grew up in and the same order of adopted personalities in children.

Though strikingly predictive of attitudes as a statistical matter, sibling birth order cannot be used to predict adopted personality types in any specific family. In fact it can act as a self-fulfilling prophecy that proves nothing if we assume that our first child will be the most academically driven, the second the most athletic and the third the most inspirational.

It is worth emphasizing that analyzing who our kids are, where they are going, why they do what they do and what they think about us is not half as important, for our sake or theirs, as understanding where *we* are coming from, who *we* are and which way *we* need to move to like ourselves better as parents.

Your Independence Program | 8

To achieve independence for yourself and your children from the patterns and pain of co-dependency, the most successful people pursue recovery on three fronts. First, seek out those who affirm your right to be the best parent you can be. Second, find inspiration in the words of the teachers who have shared spiritual truths for millennia. And third, carry on a daily personal introspection program in relationship to your child that will build your self-esteem and your connection with your child, in an ascending spiral of good feeling and love.

Fellowship

It is by sharing with others with similar experience that we learn we have value. By sharing with people who appreciate whatever little we think we have just as people, we can watch our sense of self-worth grow.

This is the special province of self-help groups, from Tough Love for parents with troublesome teens, to Al-Anon and its related 12-Step groups like Parents Anonymous, to La Leche League for breast-feeding mothers.

We need to seek out those people who will appreciate sharing our sufferings and our strengths and even our little daily triumphs and disappointments as we move toward independence.

Soon we will learn that our value is not in our suffering so much as in our attitude toward it. It is not our pain that makes us strong. Otherwise we would be merely exchanging old devices like perfectionism for new ones like self-righteousness over wrongs we've suffered.

Our value to others is our spiritual core, that essential spark of life that allows us to move through our pain, to accept hope, to share it with others, to be uniquely ourselves.

In the Hallmark Hall of Fame presentation, "My Name is Bill W.," about the founder of Alcoholics Anonymous, James Woods as Bill W. discovered that only by "talking to another drunk" could he keep himself sober. In knowing that someone else would listen and empathize with his deepest secrets, he felt that he was worth fighting the daily battle for.

Similarly as parents we can seek out others who are struggling to overcome the same challenges, and we can gain strength by helping them to rebuild their self-esteem and have faith in their progress.

We can also seek the fellowship of our children, who touch the child within us. Without burdening them with the details of our past, we can enjoy their human fellowship and validate each other, with fun, learning and sharing together.

Spiritual Inspiration And Wisdom

Recovery involves a spiritual process that is not unique to chemical dependency or co-dependency. It is the process of freeing yourself from maladaptive habits that make your happiness seem to depend on people, places and things beyond your control. All through the ages, philosophers, prophets and thinkers in diverse areas of life have given their thoughts on this process. I urge you to use their spiritual guidance for your recovery.

It is a process that continues for life and is truly no more and no less than the process of affirming life, of creating rather than destroying, of living rather than dying.

If we had nothing identifiable to recover from, we might call it enlightenment, transformation, spiritual growth. When we have an identifiable history of emotional distortion during our most impressionable time of life, the spiritual journey stands in higher relief. There are clearer milestones.

For this reason you may find people who, advanced in their recovery, express gratitude for the path their trials as children set them on. You may come to feel this same gratitude too when you have let go of past injuries and forgiven others and yourself.

So often in analysis or just sharing with friends, we are asked to acknowledge our pain, and we begin to feel its intensity, but it will not release. In fact, it may be a greater burden than when it was hidden because we are so aware of our faults now that we watch ourselves and blame ourselves for everything. Such well meant help can lead us into a deeper despair without ever leading us into recovery.

One Vietnam war veteran wrote his story about dealing with his post-war issues through analysis and then becoming a psychologist himself to help others. After 10 years, he realized he was not recovering at all. Then he discovered his spiritual gap and came to terms with his pain, which he said had predated the war. And he bemoaned that in all his years of analysis and practice, he had never heard a word about forgiveness, the key to his recovery and to the recovery of millions of others.

We need to forgive ourselves and others we have blamed to free our spirits to live today and each day as best we can.

Recovery allows us to find our path to happiness within, connecting to others without struggle because our spiritual value is not dependent on them. We become ever more independent of any force, person, place or thing outside ourselves, any attachment, as the eastern sages call it.

We do it gradually by becoming ever more directly connected with the universal life force as it waits for us in every tree, rock, shell, friend, stranger, aging parent or child.

We can draw strength and inspiration too from connecting with some of the many wonderful works of spiritual thought that have been written down through the ages and into modern times.

This necessary step of connecting has a special application for parents. We have the unique privilege of making connection with a most significant other — our child — and of experiencing day by day right in our own home how very useful we all are to each other as independent spiritual beings.

Daily Introspection: Rewriting History

You can rewrite history if you can accept that personal history, like all history, is largely a matter of interpretation.

Mind experts believe that virtually all our experiences are recorded in our minds. Before they are "filed" away, every one of them was processed through a matrix of prior interpreted experience. This process preserves our sanity, maintains some order in recall and association and makes our experience retrievable to guide us when making new choices and interpretations.

When we reach new spiritual insight such as dealing with the issues of adult children raising children, we can go back and pull out old tapes and records that contain these interpretations and rewrite them or refile them as need be in light of new information or clarity.

For example, perhaps whenever something doesn't come out exactly as you expect, you remember a phrase your father used to say like, "You dummy." You filed those memories under "What I Should Expect of Myself," not knowing anything about the destructive behavior of addicts and co-dependents.

Now you can refile that tape under "Sad Things a Loving Father Can Do Unconsciously When He Is Fighting Addiction Without Help" and never think of it again.

Or you can file it under "Reasons to Have Compassion for Addicts and Their Co-dependents." There, it will have no more effect at all on your image of yourself but can make you more compassionate and helpful to others.

You have the power to do this for yourself, and no one else does. You don't even have to say a word to your parents or others, to write a word to them, to do anything particular or different towards them, to get any particular information, answers, admissions or acceptance from them. You don't even need to have them alive anymore on this earth for your healing to take place.

Introspection works if . . .

1. You are patient with yourself.
2. You act "as if." Begin acting in your everyday life as if the healing were taking place.
3. You resist counting on or expecting anyone else to notice. (The less you count on it, the more likely it is that they will.)

The Parent-Child Bond As Experiential Laboratory

Children are the most powerful affirmation anywhere that we are creative, important, needed beings. To paraphrase Ralph Waldo Emerson, they are a powerful sign that God still has faith in us.

The parent-child bond is as pure, direct and essential as any spiritual bond can be. It is no accident that this bond is the universal metaphor for the relationship between human and Creator.

There are no secrets between parent and child that matter. If one is not completely there in spirit for the other, the other knows it.

It is our defenselessness, our sharing, our humor, our love that puts us on the path to independence. We come to accept that it is not our child, any more than it was ultimately to be our parents, our spouse, our boss or our best friend, who is responsible to make us happy. It is up to us and we have the power. Through our willingness to share ourselves with our child and others, we experience happiness.

Leading Questions

Some basic questions to lead you through your independence program are summarized below. In the chapters that follow you will learn more about how they can work for you.

1. Are there areas of your life as a parent that are chronically disturbing to you without an obvious source for the stress?
2. Were you exposed to addictive or co-dependent behavior in your childhood home?
3. What key area — touching and affection, performance and mistakes, teaching and authority, or trust and maturity — gives you the most trouble in your parenting?
4. What is your typical emotional reaction in this key sensitivity area — sense of failure and rejection, anger and defensiveness, distance and manipulation, or depression and despair?
5. Which stage of co-dependency in your family of origin is responsible for your feelings?
6. What changes do you need to make in your childhood interpretation of that stage in light of your adult knowledge and understanding?
7. What new, more genuine, functional and life-affirming responses can you now use in that key area of your parenting?

Steps To Independence

Here is an outline of the steps you can take to let go of your childhood and become the adult you want to be for your children:

1. Identify a parenting situation that frequently bothers you, such as your child's lack of respectful language, reluctance to achieve at school, self-destructive behavior, your own yelling or pleading or difficulty making decisions affecting the child.

2. Identify your feelings, both superficial and undercurrent, such as anger, frustration, hopelessness, rejection, jealousy, self-pity, self-doubt, determination.

3. Let yourself feel your feelings one at a time without judging them and listen for any old thoughts, rules, attitudes or voices (of old authority figures) that left you with messages about yourself, children or parent-child interactions and gave rise to your feelings.

4. Use the particular key area and stage of co-dependency to help you focus in on the specific message that is presently causing you trouble.

5. Identify what was going on at the time you registered this message and reconsider it in light of your deeper understanding of your parents' condition and your own childhood survival responses.

6. Articulate precisely how you want to change the imprint or tape of this message, keeping in mind your essential value as parent to your child.

7. Let new feelings flow directly from this new message, such as parental pride, hope, faith, affection, sadness, self-forgiveness, forgiveness of parents, happiness, release, nurturing to the hurt child within, tenderness and love for your child.

8. Try to notice when you enter this key area again, remind yourself of your new affirmative message and repeat it to yourself. Feel your new feelings and enjoy them.

9. Notice any change in your response by word or deed and take time to experience any self-affirming feelings your observations bring you. (If you notice no change, be patient with yourself. It will come, usually after three tries.)

10. Cultivate your personal gratitude for any changes you notice in the way your child responds to you after your changed response. (Children often need up to six different instances of changed response to begin to put down their defenses.)

11. Discuss with your child what is happening between you, to the extent you are comfortable. You can press gently and non-threateningly for their feedback, but if they are not ready, wait until another time.

12. Repeat this process for any parenting challenge.

13. Ask the child if he or she has any suggestions for other areas you can work on together to change your interactions for the better.

14. Periodically review your progress and build on the feedback loop you will discover. As you see your progress, your self-esteem will grow, and as your self-esteem grows, you will progress more quickly.

Replacing Fear With Love

In recovery we end the vicious cycle of low self-esteem as parents, and we learn to replace our fear with love.

Only if we free ourselves from fear can we live totally in the present, where love is given and received.

Guilt is fear of the past. We anticipate that at any time, punishment for our past wrongs may jump out from around the corner. We may come to fear our children because they may be, after all, the monstrous result of our ancient, supposed wrongs that we most fear.

Now we can replace guilt with its twofold antidote, forgiveness and changed behavior. Without recovery, we do not forgive because self-blame supports the credibility of our parents and protects us from the reality of their rejection. And, without recovery, we do not know how to change our behavior because of the learning disability of co-dependency.

But with recovery, we can lighten our load of guilt by forgiving, and we can begin early to feel the benefits by taking action with changed behavior.

Taking action, however small, puts us experientially in the present and gives us greater courage to let go of the past.

Worry is fear of the future. As parents we have a great excuse to spend time trying to imagine everything that might go wrong and to spend endless hours trying to assure that it doesn't. Without recovery, our spiritual gap keeps us from any faith in the future and our upside down view of our power makes us try to control others instead of ourselves.

With recovery, we have such intense pleasure in the present that we are willing to let the future take care of itself, confident that our actions today, in harmony with our positive attitudes, will build a good foundation for tomorrow.

Anxiety is fear of the present. It is the source of our urgency. We fear that at any moment we may be doing something, or leaving something undone, that will lead to disaster by letting the past catch up with us, or by setting traps for us in the future. Without recovery, we can have love all around us and not notice.

With recovery, we look for serenity within and in our human connections to crowd out our anxiety.

I find it helpful to remember this simple definition of love: *Finding the good in others and enjoying it.* If we live in fear, we look only for threats and dangers. We only steal our moments of joy at the expense of guilt, worry and anxiety.

To let go of fear, we must forgive our past and trust our future. We must forgive our parents and trust our kids.

Trusting The Healthy Natural Order Of Things

Your independence program begins soundly with the premise that your child is meant to be physically dependent on you in order to be educated into life, love and the culture that is essential to his survival.

The child is not a burden or a reluctant prisoner. He grasps the essential usefulness of the relationship. He is another human being, a bit less experienced, who appreciates and requires not your skills, your money, your experiences, your sacrifice or your devices so much as your essential self. Your job, should you accept it, is to find that essential self and share it with your child.

Your independence program is not an independence from anyone or anything. It is independence with. In the realm of the spirit, parent and child can share independence together.

In the next several chapters, we will build our independence and recovery by making a compassionate inventory of our parenting styles with the help of a closer look at the various reactions we have adopted as a result of our particular stage of childhood codependency.

From Rejection
To Affection

9

If we find our parenting style troubled by thoughts of "if only," by feelings of helplessness, powerlessness, got to's and fear of being alone or rejected, then we may be stuck in the rejection stage.

This first stage of co-dependency has the most profound effect on our ability to love and be loved.

When we come into the world as infants, the parent-child bond is expressed graphically on the physical level. The infant is a physical product of its mother and its parents' union. The umbilical cord is assumed to have mystical power in most cultural traditions: We as babies have been part of our mother's body. We touch her intimately throughout pregnancy, birth and if we are lucky, a long natural breastfeeding and weaning period of several years.

Our natural and rightful expectation is a gradual letting go over the next 15 years, with our childhood needs met by our family and immediate community. We are programmed to count on, to enjoy and to thrive on parental love and filial affection.

Blocks To Bonding

But this has not been the pattern in recent years.

A generation ago childbirth was considered a negative experience, to be blotted from memory by painkillers and anesthesia. A whole generation or two of mothers completely missed the incredible high of human connection that is afforded by the birth experience.

The increased incidence of birth by Caesarian section is the bugaboo of childbirth for a new generation of mothers, detracting from the positive boost to self-esteem that a natural birth can give. Anesthesia, lingering pain and days or weeks of disability make it harder to appreciate the amazing positive creative force of the birth experience mother and baby share.

In that time from birth to weaning, the human bond can mean as much to the mother as it does to the baby and most women who have breastfed report a unique experience of their own self-worth.

Fathers are not left out of this powerful experience. If the father has been physically involved in the birth or the pregnancy, with affectionate touching, massage, shared breathing exercise and so forth, he has had the chance to appreciate that his wife needs him just for himself, more than she needs house, paycheck, groceries, gifts or compliments.

When the current generation of adult children now raising children was born, this scenario of family-centered birth was almost non-existent in corporate, mobile, modern America.

In the 1940s and '50s, coming home from World War II, veterans wanted to adjust to peace, get a good job, forget death, courage, blood-curdling fear and the guilt of survivorship. There were parts of themselves they didn't want to share with wives, parents or buddies, much less their children. They left the babies for their wives to care for and set about creating a home for them.

In fact, many adult children raising children today may have been born when their fathers were overseas in fear for their lives. No close beginnings there!

Our mothers too were trying to forget the war, the separation, the fears. They wanted a home, a bastion of security, where no one could take their man away again. Even if he was a drunk, they held on fast. Keeping the family together by hook or crook was their deepest goal.

They often saw their babies as a way of legitimizing their choice to marry a serviceman against parental advice, or as a way of solidifying the family, or as a way to look forward, to forget the fears and separations of war.

I often wonder whether we did not lose a whole generation of wonderful people as parents by the after-effects of World War II. The silence that most of us respected about our parents' experiences was symbolic of the distance that people can put between each other as the result of the strains of war.

Today, with psychology more sophisticated now than it was after World War II, we read reams about the after-effects of Vietnam. Drug abuse, lack of ambition, spiritual vacuum are common. Some blame these effects on the absence of moral support in that particular war.

But for every veteran of Vietnam who has compromised his life and his family with drugs, I would wager there are two alcoholics who saw duty in World War II or Korea.

The Technological Family

Be that as it may, as a result of the war's shot in the arm to industry, modern technology took quantum leaps and became a new source of hope for humanity. Scientific ways of raising babies became fashionable, and modern Americans, especially after the advent of television, moved away from patterns of physical affection they had known in their ethnic families in favor of a more progressive picture.

Weighing a baby on a cold steel scale was considered more useful than bouncing her on your knee to experience her health and growth. Artificial milk, scientifically formulated, was considered more reliable than the unscientific product of the mother's body.

Our parents sought sterile environments, clean homes, objectively verifiable indications of progress in raising their children. Lots of touching, eating with the hands, sharing beds, carrying on the hip or back, all seemed inconceivable to the modern mom.

Though voices like Benjamin Spock's stood out advocating letting childhood progress naturally with as little worry as possible, even he was partly and temporarily seduced by the idea that children did not need as much touching and love as our grandmothers seemed to think they did.

In addition, economics played a part. Even in the cold era of Victorian morality nannies were there for many to touch and hug the children. After the war, they were gone.

Even a hundred years ago, it was known that a mysterious disease in orphanages and foundling homes called "failure to thrive" could be prevented by lots of physical touching and affection between caretaker and children. Often, however, there were not enough caretakers to go around.

Yet it is not too much of an exaggeration to say that the generation to which today's adult children raising children belong was largely raised with inadequate touching and affection, even though usually at least one parent was at home.

The Extra Burden Of Co-dependency

This loss was even greater in any household affected by alcoholism. As we have seen, dependency takes control of the addicted parent and isolates him or her from loved ones. Then the other family members become increasingly preoccupied with the addicted parent's altered behavior and any child is left more and more to himself.

To a baby these developments translate into rejection. A parent doesn't always come as soon as the baby calls. Touching and affection stop as soon as an upset baby is calmed. Eye contact from either parent is severely reduced, so severe is the shame they feel. Carrying is reduced, if for no other reason than that the dependent parent needs his hands to hold a glass and the co-dependent parent needs hands too, to do the extra work the dependent parent no longer does.

Loneliness, rejection and abandonment are the first negative feelings the child of an alcoholic experiences.

Born with an inherent presumption of the parents' capacity to love, the child will not at first accept abandonment. As long as she is healthy, she will scream and as she becomes older, she will adopt all kinds of other mechanisms, usually unconsciously, to get parental attention. Possibilities include hypochondria, colic, belligerence, playground accidents, intersibling rivalry, spiteful words and so forth.

Primal Need

Some parents suppose that these are the same as manipulations. But this is a common error. These are not conscious strategies to get what she wants. Instead they are direct physical results of parental rejection, primal screams as it were, a direct attempt to reach the parent, to be heard.

There can even be direct physical results of parental rejection.

1. Stress reduces immunity and increases susceptibility to disease.
2. Chronic fear and anxiety reduce digestive capacity, leading to colic, malnutrition, metabolic imbalance, allergy.
3. Reduced confidence and self-esteem increase accident proneness.
4. Chronic guilt over parental rejection can lead to physical pain, fight or flight response, violence in word and action.

Hospital nurses have told me that a child who cries when given a shot or when handled by a nurse is more likely to have a speedy recovery than one who takes it without protest. They say that this protest, implying the expectation that times should be better, often predicts quicker healing.

In a healthy family the child never doubts that his needs will be met because the parent has been ready at any time to share herself with her child as the need arises. But in co-dependency, a child may have doubts almost from birth, depending upon to what extent the addiction has taken hold.

Anthropologist Richard Leakey tells a story of the !Kung people, a tribal people who still live by hunting and gathering. Now exposed to agriculture and civilization, it was assumed they would jump at the chance to settle down. But when asked why they did not embrace the new way of life more eagerly, an elder said, to paraphrase, "It's too hard. Here, all the nuts we need fall from the trees of the forest and all the food we need is provided by our forest. Why build houses and grow food?"

A child whose parents' attention is centered on their dependency lacks this kind of faith in the universe to provide. And with good reason.

Now when this child has his own children, it is little wonder he does not know how to show his parental affection and is more likely to focus his attention on getting it, not giving it.

Options For Affection

You may decide to straddle the fence between parenting instinct and childhood training. You may decide to show more affection than your parents did while taking care not to go crazy or spoil the child. It seems a good compromise that won't raise eyebrows or bring too many risks to your own equilibrium.

But you are likely to find that these happy compromises do not make the child happy. When they don't work, you may pull back, listening to old tapes about spoiling and letting the child run your life.

Instead, you may have to give yourself a push forward.

Meagan

Meagan, an adult child raising children, had developed a compromise of letting the baby sleep in her room, in a bassinet by the bed. A cradle in the next room seemed too distant, but sharing a bed seemed altogether primitive. People only did that who couldn't afford a nice crib, right?

The baby thought otherwise. After weeks of sleepless nights trying to sit up nursing and then lay him down again to sleep just when he would wake up again, Meagan turned off all the old tapes and closed all the books.

Her solution was to ask herself what a mother cat would do.

She lay down in bed, put her baby beside her and let him do what he wanted all along. They slept happily and long together.

The Primacy Of The Parent-Child Bond

With our own children, we must begin slowly, one step at a time, to establish a physical bond and to express our own parental love openly.

We must keep in mind that we are lovable to our children solely because we are their parents. No matter what our past mistakes, neglects, failures, misconceptions, this is so.

As parent and child, we can relearn physical affection together. We need not perfect it before we share it.

The first step is to use words to express our changing attitudes. We might say something like this.

"You know, when I was a child, my parents didn't do much hugging or kissing because of the way they were raised, their personal beliefs or the things on their mind at different stages of my childhood. (If they are old enough, which is younger than you think, by all means talk about their addiction.) But I think I would have liked it if I had had more hugs. I think I'll give you a hug more often, okay?"

This will work with children of any age.

Michael

Michael was the father of a 17-year-old girl who had lived with her mother abroad for 10 years and came to him for her last two years of high school. He was distressed that in a year he felt no closer to her. Son of an alcoholic, he had had little affection as a child and was unaware he had missed it.

Michael began to offer an occasional hug to his daughter, after sharing his own experience with her. She seemed uninterested in the tales of her alcoholic grandfather and Michael felt rebuffed.

But he kept with the suggestions of more touching and tried stroking an arm, brushing a cheek. He was delighted to find that in a matter of weeks she was giving him hugs before leaving for school, patting his shoulder when sitting on the couch and, most important, giving him the feeling that he really mattered to her and that she knew she really mattered to him.

Negative Touching

Often adult children's principal memory of touching is not affectionate but punishing, like spankings. The line, if there is one, between spankings and abuse, is a fine one.

Never having absolutely decided against an occasional spanking, I have never come upon a time in my parenting when I thought it would be the least bit useful or meaningful in any way.

Since in all this time an appropriate occasion has never arisen, I have come to believe that it is without any rational basis. To reach this belief, I have had to accept that my parents were mistaken in even the occasional spankings I received and to forgive them for it and forgive myself for believing I deserved it.

If you let yourself explore a similar process, you are likely to find that aggressive touching of a child seldom, if ever, has a constructive purpose or motivation and serves no short or long-term goal without an unacceptable price.

Both threatening punishment and withholding punishment out of mercy are as dangerous as giving punishment in terms of the burden of guilt we pass on to our children. The practice can lead to self-punishment as well, as a guilt avoidance mechanism.

If failures of our children make us want to punish, we must consider whether we are motivated by anger at negative reflections on ourselves as parents.

If we deal with this anger with the tools in this book, we can move on to love and affection.

Guilt, Forgiveness And Love

A powerful commentary appears in one of the books used in Al-Anon. It explains the spiritual idea that we have no right to judge others. It tells how forgiving is a way of letting go of others' wrongs. But how do we know if they are wrong if we haven't judged, the commentator wonders. If we never judged, we would have nothing to forgive.

So ultimately it is only ourselves we must forgive, for having wronged another by judging them.

This is a profound idea for the adult children raising children. If as adults we feel we have forgiven our parents and yet we are troubled by continuing guilt, chances are we have not yet forgiven ourselves for not loving our parents despite their wrongs. For judging them in the first place and for not knowing any better, we need to be forgiving to the child we once were.

Early Abandonment

Many adult children raising children report nightmares that they have forgotten their child somewhere or abandoned them. These are reverberations of our own fear of abandonment.

Even if you were never abandoned, you need to consider whether you were exposed to any threats or periods of separation. Talk of divorce, threats to leave you screaming in the supermarket and even a week-end separation for a vacation trip can be enough, together with the underlying loneliness and sense of emotional abandonment of being a child of co-dependency, to create a fear of abandonment that persists into your life as a parent.

The Touchstone Of Reality

Once we have learned what mistaken conclusions give rise to our estrangement of parental affection, our guilt and our aggressive outbursts, we must replace them with conclusions based in reality.

Reality is not established by majority vote. We may notice that many children resent their parents, feel alienated or abandoned at times, feel guilty and don't know how to take a hug. We may perceive that most parents spank their children, feel uncomfortable offering hugs and are reluctant to be vulnerable around their children, assuming there are always secrets between parent and child.

But this does not mean that this is the reality of the parent-child relationship. Marcus Aurelius said that what has been done, can be done. If one parent-child couple you know or know of has an easygoing, physically affectionate, guilt-free and candid attitude, then you can too.

Sex

Any touchy subject can be manipulated by an addicted parent and lead to misinterpretations in the co-dependent family. Sex is a prime example. Often co-dependents assume that all physical touching has some threat and that there is always a sexual overtone because of misleading messages from their troubled parents.

Often these messages were rationalizations for the absence of affectionate touching in co-dependent families. With this interpretation, you can quickly develop guilt over all urges to hug, kiss, hold hands, rest together and so forth.

Confusion about sexuality, how to take flirtation and how to distinguish friends from lovers are rampant among adult children raising children. Our children, in turn, can develop a fear of strangers, a fascination with sex, alienation from their bodies and more, by the misleading messages we pass on.

These interpretations need to be replaced with a recognition that our bodies are not solely instruments of sex or aggression. They are first and foremost our personal homes. They are instruments of touch and affection in all kinds of relationships, as we choose, not the least of which is parent-child.

Taking the risk of affection is the greatest challenge in overcoming the wounds we carry from the stage of rejection. Opening up to a child is a healing process that begins and ends with you.

In the childhood home, parents often cover over the gaps in parental affection by inventing specific reasons for withholding love. The adult child hears echoes of these: her unworthiness, failure to achieve, untrustworthiness, thoughtlessness, laziness or stupidity are always easy targets.

Or our parents attached strings to moments of affection, again with no harm intended but with harm inflicted. Perhaps your father waxed sentimental and affectionate when he reached a certain stage in a drinking binge. Perhaps your mother gave most of her hugs when she was feeling desperate and looked to you to bolster her spirits.

These negative associations with physical affection can get in your way when you try to express your own parental love.

Having internalized your parents' patterns of withholding love, inventing excuses or using affection as a reward or to meet their co-dependency needs, we not only have trouble giving unconditional love. We also can be confused, angry or overcome with guilt, unworthiness, urgency or impostor feelings when we receive it from our children.

How many parents immediately think of a hundred things they need to get done just when a child wants to snuggle down for a while?

Again we must check our self-esteem and affirm that as the spiritual beings we are, beneficiaries of the gift of children, we deserve their love.

Seek Out Models Of Affection

Seek out people and groups who help you experience unqualified praise and appreciation just for being you. At first you will distrust it, believing it is a show, a superficial pat on the back that can't possibly solve your deepest concerns. But give it a chance.

Stay away as long as necessary from any neighbors, siblings, parents, in-laws, secretary or anyone else who judges or criticizes you as a parent instead of taking joy in your successes and encouraging you in your weak areas.

Hang around families who do have an easy-going pattern of hugs, strokes, kisses, climbing, carrying, eye contact, playful wrestling and cuddling. Let your child see it too.

Begin slowly and let the good feelings flow. It is these that build your self-esteem as a parent.

Fears of rejection that may have plagued you for years can be replaced by faith in the invincibility of parent-child love.

Filial Affection And Suppression Of Love

In a very real sense, co-dependency can be viewed as the result of suppressed love. When your parent cannot receive the love you felt for him or her, the energy of your love must go somewhere. It disperses in numerous directions, trying to force love, deny it, pretend you have it or transform it into power, control, worry, hate and more.

The only cure is to learn to love again and to let go of all substitutes for filial affection. Yet many adult children have no comprehension of the term. It sounds merely antique and inapplicable.

Having been denied any practice in healthy human touch and affection, it is no wonder that they are not good at it now. And their love, suppressed, oozes out instead in strange forms like, "Wish he'd stay a baby forever," or criticizing, gifts, judging, worrying, overprotecting and killing with kindness.

Now we can begin with our children to love purely and simply, by reaching out a hand, by letting our eye rest on theirs, by giving a kiss in the morning or by taking a hand when you pass each other in the hall.

Love is built one precious moment at a time.

From Defenses To Self-Expression | 10

If you find yourself constantly checking on your child, demanding to hear plans, excuses and apologies, criticizing and calling names and finding frequent fault with his behavior, you are most likely stuck in the defenses stage of co-dependency.

This second stage dominates the key sensitivity area of your child's performance and mistakes. While you are still trying to defend your own worthiness against old tapes of parental criticism, your high standards put your child on the defensive, constantly feeling challenged to prove his competence.

If angry attack and parry seem a chronic pattern between you, you will need to learn to speak and act from yourself — not to prove anything to anyone but only to express your spiritual being.

Defenses are predicated on the underlying assumption that if we were really who we are supposed to be — who our parents wanted us to be or expect us to be or who we are truly capable of being, somewhere in the realm of perfection, we suspect — life would be good. Our ultimate goal is somehow to please our parents and get the promised rewards for doing so.

The defenses are designed to prove and convince both our parents and ourselves that we are worthy of love and attention. Or we may use them to hide the fact that we are not worthy. We try to please our parents and bolster them in their ability to meet our needs, as we strive to prove we have earned their love.

As parents, we think we know the rules as we gleaned them from childhood, but when the roles are changed, with us now as the parents, none of it makes any sense any more.

Results don't occur as we would have predicted from our prior beliefs. We try to act as we wanted so much to have our parents act and we are dumbfounded to find that our children are still using defenses against us just as we did with our parents.

The path out of this chronic parental frustration is to identify our own defenses, confront the underlying self-doubts that they are camouflaging, and begin relating to our children as independent people, not as threats, competitors, burdens, challenges, authorities, charity cases, etc.

We need to learn to speak from the heart, to speak for ourselves and about our feelings, and to act as we are moved by our heartfelt self, not according to one or another of the scripts we learned long ago.

We need to be patient with our children as they begin to notice that our defenses are down and adjust by letting down theirs. We need to share the process of this healing, to let them know what is going on, to help them understand why we are changing and to model positive change for them.

We must be on our toes not to turn our sharing into a burden. Remind yourself that your children cannot be responsible to meet the needs of your inner child any more than we could meet the needs of our own parents, try as we might.

Vance

Vance's son, Jeff, was driving him crazy and he suspected it was him. A single parent, he knew he had serious issues of his own childhood to work out, but the tantrums and rebelliousness of his son kept him so preoccupied that he feared he would become abusive before he ever found time to deal with his own issues. So he sought help for parenting, not thinking of help for himself.

"Jeff's a good kid and I want nothing more than for him to be happy and to get along with him. But ever since he turned three — he's almost ten now — even before the divorce, he's got on my nerves so easily I feel like hitting him.

"Like when we are at home in the evening, he'll refuse to clean up his stuff, which is all over the living room. I try to be kind and understanding, but I can't stand when his stuff takes over the house and he knows that. But he'll say he's going to do it and he never does until I am yelling, swearing, calling him names and throwing his stuff in the wastebasket."

Vance's parenting issues reflected the stage of defenses in his childhood home. Anger and frustration dominated his reactions to his child.

What Are We Defending, Against What Or Whom?

Defense is more than a catch-all word used for all the mildly to seriously irrational, troublesome things we do in reaction to our daily life.

Defenses are barricades we erect in order to protect our fragile self-image against others' expectations, judgments and criticisms of us. They are also erected against our own judgments of ourselves that we impose through the perverted logic that follows ignorance of the nature of our parents' dependency.

Fighting Yourself

It is painful to realize that all our well-developed defenses are really defenses against ourselves. It is a simple spiritual truth that ultimately defenses are only against ourselves. If we did not accept someone else's judgment as true at least to some extent, we would need no defense against it. After all, we know that words can never hurt us unless we let them. If we defend against someone else's judgment then we are really defending against our own acceptance of the other's judgment.

Many of us have spent most of our lives defending against others' judgments, parrying disparagements, striving to prove ourselves better than they thought, protesting unfairness and discrimination against us for our supposed unworthiness, arguing away complaints and criticisms, trying to whittle down unreasonable expectations of parents, boss, spouse.

But in this realization that all defenses are against ourselves is the seed of a solution. If the complaints of others were our problem, we would be smack up against the spiritual truth that we cannot force others to do what we want or to change their ways. Others have the freedom to say whatever they want. But we have the freedom not to listen. If our acceptance of others' judgments of us is our problem, we do have power to change this.

10 Defense Clusters

Keeping in mind that we are defending against harsh judgment of ourselves, here is a summary of 10 frequent defenses.

Exact classifications do not matter here as much as subjective recognition, suggestive interpretations, descriptive metaphors, personal identifications, that can stimulate a feeling of "Ah-hah, that's one too!"

1. **Guilt.** I blame myself for my own and others' problems. I expect less of myself because of this and watch myself to see if it is true. It can make me chronically self-conscious, clumsy, hesitant, fearful, apologetic and mistake-prone.
2. **Self-limitation.** I assume that I am not all I might dream of so I fight my natural inclinations, which I see as unrealistic. I make things hard for myself, assuming that success requires struggle and effort. I believe that value comes from fighting external forces and from personal discomfort, sacrifice of self and strife.
3. **Analysis.** I try to understand everything, analyzing situations and people until I'm exhausted. I try to force everything into making sense, following some logical scheme which I impose.
4. **Rule-making.** I make rules for different situations and try to follow them. I make rules for others and try to hold them to them and condemn them if they fail to see their necessity or to obey them. I protest all inconsistency, indecision, hypocrisy, unfairness, breach of duty and broken promises. I overlook my own inconsistencies when I break my own rules, particularly when I am trying to get others to comply with the rules that I decide are most important.
5. **Use of force.** I use intimidation and urgency to get my way, screaming, threatening, yelling orders, acting desperate or suicidal. I create crises by making trouble, increasing the stakes, taking unnecessary risks, getting all the attention on me.
6. **Best defense.** I defend by offense, finding fault, passing judgment, criticizing, complaining, placing blame, condemning. I keep records in my head, keep score of past wrongs, assess the relative seriousness of offenses, escalate conflicts, deny any personal fault, blame, causation or contribution. I use denial as more than just the disbelief of an abandoned child. It becomes a defensive way of life.

7. **Withdrawal**. I act independent, making my decisions without consultation or consideration. I act uncaring and avoid sharing or interacting about anything except necessary superficialities. I stay away from situations that make me uneasy, letting others rescue me and carry my ball or pick up my pieces. I avoid challenges and take on as little responsibility as possible. I act totally reliable in the small manageable realm and totally unreliable in everything else. I cultivate preoccupation.

8. **Overachievement**. I am determined to perform at top level at all times so I will never feel guilty again. I am constantly on view, if not to others then to myself, always performing and watching for mistakes. I am always proving or demonstrating something to others or myself. I make superhuman effort to do my duty, to please others, to get approval, to achieve perfection and to earn sympathy when my impossible standards are not achieved. I require the same high performance of others.

9. **Fantasy**. I exaggerate my successes, minimize, hide and deny my mistakes, beat myself mercilessly over missed opportunities and forget to enjoy my achievements. I avoid sharing my feelings or activities on a long list of forbidden topics and fill the gap with silence, trivialities, dramatizations or what I think my listener wants to hear.

10. **Departure from self**. I judge myself by outside standards, having no faith in my own judgment or in any direct connection between me and any source of goodness, abundance and hope in my life. I have given up on myself, feeling only anger towards myself when I allow myself to think about me. I look to books, experts and free advice, collecting justifications for my actions. I am an advice shopper, pitting one bit of advice against another, meanwhile complaining of lack of time, money, energy or expertise to make any particular solution work. I speak in shoulds, ought-tos, musts, have-tos and why-don't-yous.

Just about everyone has used these defenses at some time. Defenses do serve a purpose. They allow us to fend off attack long enough to reassert our protective self-esteem and walk away from hurtful words or actions. But adult children raising children may lack the ability to walk away and one defense leads to another in endless escalation while we lap up all the negative messages about ourselves. In this context, the defenses become chronic, inappropriate and harmful to a healthy parent-child interaction.

In particular, defenses we developed as children in a co-dependent family situation get in the way of healthy parent-child interaction when we are adults raising our own children.

Experiment With Defenselessness

Your laboratory for experimenting with freedom from defenses will be your everyday interactions with your child.

If your child raises any kind of defense, your first inclination may be to complain about it, state some rule that outlaws its being used, raise some threat of punishment or other consequence or give a command against it.

All the while you may feel guilty and angry because the very emotions and defenses you could not control in yourself are certainly going to be beyond your control in your child. Fear becomes an ever present feeling, which you suppress and hide from yourself.

Becoming defenseless calls for a completely different sequence of thoughts and responses. If your child raises a defense, you need to take a moment to breathe and to think. Then you might ask yourself these questions.

1. "What is he or she reacting to in me?"
2. "What feeling have I projected and where did it come from?"
3. "Does it relate to the situation at hand or does its nature, intensity or tenacity stem from past experiences unrelated to my child?"
4. "How can I express my true self to my child at this moment, free of feelings and attitudes carried over from past experiences of my own, unrelated to him or her?"

Patterns For Building Self-Expression

There are useful patterns of speech that can help us learn to express ourselves instead of ·playing some role assumed as a defense years ago. If you practice following them in your speech, you will discover that only you can fill in the blanks. If you now use patterns for which anyone else can fill in the blanks, then you need to make a change.

These patterns are a way of preventing yourself from pretending you are anyone else and encouraging you to be yourself.

For example, suppose you have made a request that is reasonable in your eyes but usually meets with resistance, such as homework, job application or lawn-mowing. Here is a sample monologue:

"I am getting the impression from your words (or actions) you are feeling _____ (angry, secretive, threatened, depressed, resentful, etc.).

"I can understand your feeling. I usually feel that way when _____ (some situation in your experience close to the child's present one).

"Right now I feel _____ (uncomfortable, hurt, angry, like making more rules, rejected, helpless, disappointed, unappreciated, etc.) when you speak (or act) this way.

"Your _____ (homework, etc.) is important to me and I want to avoid repeated conflict over it.

"In the past I have acted out my old feelings when I _____ (told you what to do, yelled at you, forbade you, punished you, snapped at you, blamed you, was sarcastic, was critical, etc.).

"I would like to be more direct about my real feelings now.

"I am confident that we can work this out to the satisfaction of us both. I would like us both to be better about telling our feelings. I am going to work on it whether you do or not, but will you think about it? What do you think?"

In this monologue, you have first been candid about the message you have received from your child about his feelings.

Then you have empathized with the child's feeling, no matter how defensive and offensive it is to you. This legitimizes and validates the child as a person, free to have her feelings. Empathy has the effect of defusing built-up anxiety.

Then you have expressed your exact feelings of the moment, often a rare thing for adult child as parent.

Then you have shared something about the situation at hand.

Then you have been candid and honest about your earlier feelings that you had been hiding behind your defenses.

Then you express your desire to be more genuine next time.

You close by inviting your child to join you, an invitation that is programmatically irresistible to a child. Every gene in the collective inheritance of Man urges a child to join in his parents' activities, especially if lovingly invited. If the child's defensive habits prevent his immediate cooperation, be patient and try again soon.

Moving To Self-Expression

Here are the major elements in the defense-lowering process that allow us to set the context for meaningful expression of ourselves in any situation:

1. **Reflecting back.** You candidly acknowledge in words a message you are receiving.
2. **Empathy.** You validate the reasonableness of the child's message and her right to have whatever feeling she wants. She is then more ready to listen to you.
3. **Self-expression.** You identify exactly where you are right now on the emotional level — usually *uncomfortable* is good enough if a more exact word doesn't come to mind.
4. **De-escalation.** Having acknowledged that you both have valid feelings that are worthy of your mutual attention, you offer your feelings and goals about the particular issue at hand.
5. **Modeling defenselessness.** You identify your defensive mode and your wish to replace it with genuine communication.
6. **Expression of hope.** You express your hope and confidence that you can create a good result.
7. **Sharing.** You invite cooperation in the healing process for the benefit of your mutual relationship (not for your health nor for hers alone).

Easy Does It

Returning to Vance's case, Vance practiced a few of these scripts to himself, not sure they could ever work. Next time his son acted up, Vance did not automatically remain calm and speak from the heart. Old habits of emotion and defense are slow to change.

But he was able to recognize his own discomfort and was surprised how much awareness he could have of it, even before the exchange over picking up the room had reached a high level of noise and tension.

Next time the whole thing began again, Vance caught himself yelling, "Damn it, Jeff, I'm tired of this. Just do it!"

Jeff yelled back, "I can't," stomped his foot, and ran for the stairs to his room.

Vance took a long breath, lowered his voice, and said, "Wait a minute. We're both really upset. I can see you are really angry because I am insisting you clean up when you don't want to. I'm sorry you feel you have to yell and run away to get me to see how upset you are. I know it's because of the way I've been acting too.

"It makes me really uncomfortable when you get so upset. I get angry like that too when someone tells me what to do about my own stuff.

"Right now I feel concerned and frustrated that maybe you don't appreciate how nice it is to be neat and to have a clean house, and that you don't appreciate me, I guess, for how hard I try to have a good home for us both.

"Before I was acting out my feeling of frustration when I yelled and gave you orders. I move too quickly from concern to frustration because I often didn't know what I was supposed to do when I was a child in order to please my parents. I want to do a better job being clear with you about what I think is important for our home and ourselves.

"I am working on this. It's not easy. Any chance you could help me in this by being clearer about your feelings too? I think we could think up some new ways together to deal with this if we weren't yelling at each other."

Vance felt scared and relieved at the same time. Would Jeff think he had gone soft in the head?

He was surprised to learn that once his son heard this approach, he was quiet and thoughtful. The next time he got the same kind of message from his dad, he was quick to offer solutions, like a special time of day for clean-up, a new spot for his equipment, a fun code word for *too much mess*, and so on.

Frustration over a messy room changed from an awful restimulator of a feeling of helplessness for the parent and source of bad messages for the child into a reinforcer of mutual respect and individual self-esteem for both.

Better Self-Expression Through Better Self-Esteem

Self-esteem comes from feeling you have direct influence over the course of your life. You get this feeling when you accomplish something you set out to do in line with your highest priorities. A positive interaction with your child that you consciously helped to bring about is a powerful self-esteem builder for you. You begin to experience the wonderful feedback loop of conscious parenting:

When you express yourself clearly and honestly, you get a response that makes you feel good about yourself, and when you feel good about yourself, you find it ever easier and more enjoyable to express yourself.

Prepare And Practice

You need to prepare in your quiet times for encounters that tend to make you raise your defenses. You can often benefit by rehearsing and imagining your child's common defense reactions, how you can label their actions or feelings nonjudgmentally for empathy's sake — not for analysis — and how you can do the same for your own words and actions.

Strange as it may seem at first, we need to rehearse being ourselves.

We have had so many years to practice these defensive roles, to perfect these performances, to sling that retort, to drop that bomb, to hurl that little zinger, that we need to practice this new pattern just as if it were another role. Eventually we will break through to our real selves so that speaking from the heart comes even more "naturally" than our lifelong defenses.

The best way, and sometimes the only way, to tell the difference between an old defense and a genuine self-expression is by the way we feel. This is another reason it is so critical to get in touch with our feelings. If we are still hiding from them, we cannot use them as an indicator of how we are doing.

Genuine self-expression gives good feelings that last. Defensive reaction gives good feelings that are only momentary.

The defense gives us a temporary sense of security followed by a sense of aloneness. Self-expression gives a temporary sense of risk followed by an abiding sense of connectedness.

To recognize a defensive mode in ourselves, then, we must first pay more attention to how we feel. Our feelings are the quickest route to our inner thoughts.

If we do not lay down our defenses, ultimately they will fail. In the next stage, we experience a major shift in goals.

From Manipulation
To Communication

11

The third stage of co-dependency represents a major change in focus from the second.

In the defenses stage, the adult child raising children still believes that his family might meet his needs if only he could be smart enough, good enough, quick enough, honest enough, attractive enough, energetic enough, caring enough.

In the manipulation stage, he realizes that no matter how hard he tries to be these things or how persuasive he is about being them, the promised love won't come.

He still does not recognize that it is the addiction and other-centeredness of his parents that prevents them from meeting his needs. He still blames his own unworthiness. But his unrequited love and suppressed filial affection begin to turn to hate. He hates his family for how they make him feel.

Hate is fear coupled with blame. The manipulative child fears for his life and blames his parents for it. But to hate a parent is like a mortal sin. All cultural traditions insist we be grateful for our birth and cast no blame on our parents.

The child who gives up on his parents and hates them for it quickly find ways to hide these awful feelings and convinces himself that he doesn't need, want or have any feelings at all.

He decides that if his parents refuse to meet his needs, he can live without their love. He seeks approval elsewhere. He gets as much of his material and survival needs met as possible at home through manipulation and then goes elsewhere for everything else, if there is anything else — he's no longer sure.

He may put off marriage and go after success, money, more training or whatever he thinks will affirm for himself that he is okay without parental love. He becomes totally outer-motivated.

Limited Goals

You make a dramatic shift from demanding love in the rejection stage and defending against its absence in the defenses stage, to giving up on it entirely in the manipulative stage.

You stop trying to make your parents behave the way you think they should towards yourself or others. You merely play the games until you get what you think you need at any particular time to get by.

You learn how to manipulate primarily from your parents in your co-dependent childhood home. In this stage, the dependent parent has reached the point where he is no longer convincing in holding out the carrot of love if only you were a more pleasing child. The parent's problem is no longer just undeniable. It is becoming disabling. He now completely fades out unexpectedly, or switches gears, changes the rules of the game too often, and makes no pretense at rationality.

When the addicted parent can no longer hide his problem and can no longer put you on the defensive often enough to justify his dependency, he will use manipulation to make opportunities and excuses to drink or take his other chosen chemical. A formerly gentle, thoughtful person in this stage of addiction may turn mean and spiteful just to manipulate your feelings so as to create a quarrel and an excuse for his behavior.

This change in parental behavior can push the co-dependent child from attempts to explain and please to attempts to control.

You tend to become the child you always deplored, the one who stops home briefly to get what he needs, drops off or picks up some stuff, and then heads out. The one who calls only when you need money. The one who trades emotional favors for material assistance.

Training For Manipulation

Often an older child will stay in the defensive stage or even the rejection stage as the addiction progresses to this point, always trying to bring back the good old days.

A younger child, however, who is born into the alcoholic family when hurled insults, vitriolic exchanges and other manipulations are already a matter of course, may slip quickly into manipulative patterns that would put many adults on their ears. With no experience of loving exchanges, she has no bygone days to hanker after.

But the spiritual gap is still there. Even if the child has never known tender family moments, she will miss them deep inside. Her spiritual being will nag at her perpetually, cry out in the dark for connectedness. She will never feel right and good about herself until she asks for more out of life than to win at the games of manipulation.

Manipulating What?

We manipulate emotions. We accept that we have a gap where love might be. We convince ourselves it doesn't need filling, that love is an illusion and that happiness is easier to find without it.

We feel we have dropped romantic notions about family, love and life ourselves and we are eager to help disillusion others. Manipulation comes, then, from a very dark place.

We find ourselves playing on the other's guilt, instigating arguments, provoking anger, withdrawal or escape, inspiring sentimentality and stimulating other feelings towards specific goals.

Guilt is the preferred currency of manipulation, and we manipulate our own guilt as well as others'.

Meanwhile, we deny any feeling except perhaps pity. We tend to talk in terms of enjoyment, respect and fun in connection with our relationships with others, not love. We have persuaded ourselves that love does not exist without unacceptable strings attached.

We begin to suspect everyone who offers love and approval to us, looking for the strings, feeling manipulated ourselves. We want power and control in all our affairs, personal and business. We use warm feelings as a tool.

We are liable to have great trouble with the unabashed love and emotion of babies and children. We are likely to be among those who wish all babies were born three years old. "They're no fun until you can talk to them and teach them things," we've all heard parents say.

We may feel that preparing our child for the knocks of the world, for the tit-for-tat rules and for "no free lunch," is the most important thing we can do. Good advice will be the gift we value most for our child.

Most parental frustration in this stage comes from the key area of teaching and authority. The manipulator's basic assumptions in these areas need correction and will bring conflict until his spiritual gap is healed.

Children expect more than the parent in the manipulative stage is comfortable giving. Once the child senses that there is no love forthcoming unless it is paid for with absolute obedience, the manipulative games can begin.

Favorite Games

The manipulative games can be described any number of ways, but here are a few of the most common games families play.

1. Symbolic Behavior. We begin to use body language, voice tone and the timing of symbolic actions to communicate predetermined feelings. We use things like body stance, eyebrows and trivial actions like slamming a door or a drawer or clanking the dishes, the same way a healthy person would use words.

We avoid the exactitude and quotability of words, leaving more and more of our interactions completely dependent on interpretation.

Instead of saying, "I am getting angry because you forgot again to take out the garbage," we take up the basket, stomp with it out the door and dump it on the ground. Instead of speaking to the other about our feelings, we speak to ourselves, saying, "What can I do to show him how wrong he is? It is his fault for making me have these feelings of anger that I must now suppress."

Symbolic behavior can completely replace normal communication. In fact whole generations can go by playing the game, with everyone staying in bounds by never expressing a true contemporaneous feeling.

It becomes a vicious trap because we are always moving and taking action, and it is impossible for us to know or take responsibility for whatever other people may choose to "read into" our behavior or for what others may "mean" by their own.

We build symbolic behaviors one level upon another until the whole structure of innuendos comes tumbling down periodically, with each denying that anything was "meant by it," and leaving nothing upon which to build better understanding for next time. But the manipulator is just as happy because genuine communication would threaten his controlling grip.

When symbolic behavior dominates interaction, even our words discuss the other's behavior, never our own and never feelings.

2. Projection. We manipulate by projecting on to the other total responsibility for the way we feel and act. We may constantly watch the other and give them signals of what unacceptable emotion they may be stimulating in us. We never own up to actually having the emotion.

It is very much like the childhood game of directing another in a backyard search by hints of "hot," "cold," "cooler" and "warmer." We never quite tell them where we want them to go but we give them hints *ad nauseum.*

Instead of owning up to our anger and finding out what within us gives us that reaction, we say instead, "You made me angry last night."

Or, "You know how angry that makes me feel."

Or, "Do you want me to get angry?"

Or, "You just did that to make me angry."

Or, "Why the heck did you do that?"

Or, "Would you like it if I did that to you?"

We never just simply express our feelings. We refuse to take responsibility for our feelings, to own them. We bargain by trading accusations and apologies.

3. Rationalization. Anyone with a good mind can rationalize anything. Lawyers have raised it to a sophisticated art while politicians have become famous for it. But it is not limited to these professionals.

Time management expert Charles Hobbs describes rationalization as the thoughts we invent to cover the gap between our basic personal values and our performance. It protects our sanity so that we don't get what he calls "gappitis." But, he points out, it is a temporary solution and does not relieve the stress of having the gap.

In parenting, any gap between who we want to be and who we are is very obvious to us because we have continual feedback from our children. We can rationalize until blue in the face, but our little child will not be impressed if things are not going well between us.

With older children, we may convince them of our favorite rationalizations, but when they use them back at us for their own ends or point out a basic inconsistency between several of our favorites, our discomfort is acute.

Often our rationalizations amount to dangerous negative messages we would not deliberately impose on our children. Examples are:

- "At my age, you're too old to change."
- "You never get what you really want."
- "There's always someone out to get you." And so forth.

Often our rationalizations are inherited and we've never examined them in the light of functional reality. Now is the time.

4. *Policing For Inconsistency.* We may be entirely inconsistent in our tone, attitudes and behavior while we tell others they are not making sense because two of their behaviors cannot be rationalized together. A key manipulation, it takes all free will away from the other by implying that their choices should be transparent, predictable and patently justifiable in our eyes — a major authoritarian stance.

With children, insistence on consistency is particularly damaging because childhood is an almost constant process of play and experimentation. None of us would ever have learned anything useful if we had had to give a good explanation for everything before we did it. This contributes, no doubt, to the learning disability of co-dependency.

5. *Rules.* We insist on obedience to lines of authority and protocol. We must be obeyed, humored, loved, respected and so forth by virtue of mere trappings, like parental authority or the emperor's robe. We parent by legislation and command. We ignore the fact that reliable respect for authority must be earned and that our children owe us nothing.

Respect for parental authority is real and reliable only if built with mutual trust and sharing on the bedrock of the parent-child bond.

These five manipulative strategies can drive anyone up a wall. They account for the vast majority of manipulative behaviors throughout our lives. But no matter how successful they are at our parents' home, the office or the club, no matter how well we "play the game" in different areas of our lives, we feel empty and helpless when we use these with our kids.

Madelaine

Madelaine had tried every trick in the book to make her son, Mark, achieve at school. And it had worked. He was getting straight As. She had helped him with his homework through elementary school, giving him the best tips she knew. She had convinced him to buy only learning games, to avoid wasting time on video games and team sports that would be useless to his adult life.

She had got across to him that teachers didn't want creative thinking. They wanted you to know what they had taught, inside and out. He would take a second look at his work just if she raised an eyebrow. He knew when she was displeased just by the way she stood.

She felt that this showed what great communication they had. "We can read each other's minds." She was dumbfounded to be asked to consider if she ever communicated her feelings to him.

Madelaine sought help because teachers complained that Mark seemed to have no friends and never seemed to have any fun. She admitted that he was always manipulating her into finding entertainment for him. He didn't seem to be maturing into the confident teenager she had expected, despite his straight As.

She needed to liberate Mark from the manipulative patterns with which she had raised him. She needed to learn the difference between the manipulative projection, "You know you're hurting me by not trying your hardest," and the communication, "I feel disappointed because it seems to me you are not trying very hard."

She needed to consider the difference between saying, "I know you are going to be a great writer one day," and saying, "I love to read what you write."

She began to distinguish between judgments and personal feelings. Did she enjoy teaching him? Did she enjoy having him as her son? Had she ever told him?

She needed to be more herself and let him be more himself. She began to leave more decisions to him and to ask instead of tell. Gradually their interaction gave him a better model for communication and he began to make friends and enjoy their company.

Our Most Human Skill

Human beings are a very special species. We are designed more uniquely for communication than any species we know of. We have special abilities to give and receive messages by facial expression, hand movement, writing, spoken word and symbols.

Communication is our most distinguishing feature as human beings. It is responsible for our adaptability and our intricate social survival skills. We spend longer learning to communicate than any other species. And our learning would not be possible without communication.

We have very little hair on our faces. This means that every movement of every facial muscle is revealed to others. This is no accident.

In addition to facial expression, we also have words. We can express things that have absolutely no relationship to current experience and others will know what we mean.

With face and words, we can say one thing and express another on our face, an amazing feat no other animal can do. Finally, we have symbolic thought and imagination. We have the ability to live through an experience totally in our minds, without ever having done it. This gives us unparalleled ability to anticipate the consequences of actions, to plan ahead, to make choices and to be conscious of ourselves as active forces in our lives.

With faces, words and symbols, we can share all this with others. We are able to share our innermost experiences with others by communicating our feelings and emotions. They can understand us by imagining what we are saying in their own minds and by resonating with the same emotions that they see expressed on our faces. And they can respond.

We can affirm our spiritual connectedness with but a smile and they can do the same back.

With these abilities, we can influence each other in many ways, to cooperate, to share and otherwise to meet our mutual needs in a way that promotes voluntary cooperation and attention to community.

But when we manipulate, we are using these abilities as little more than a sophisticated substitute for brute force. This denial of our humanity cannot help but keep us unhappy, and we descend into ever more pitiful manipulations.

But Will They Listen?

Many fear expressing emotion because they confuse communication with acting out. We get trapped in the caveman picture that suggests that anger is communicated by attack.

But most anthropologists agree that human beings, and perhaps all primates, have the ability and the natural inclination to communicate feelings, aggression, status and related matters without coming to blows.

Our options are not limited to attack on the one hand or suppression of anger on the other hand.

We have many options in between because of our ability to communicate.

But like so many other human skills, communication is a learned skill. If we have not learned it by now, we need to educate ourselves.

Feelings First

True communication doesn't happen unless the two people involved have communicated on the feeling level. This is because any other sharing will be either boring or threatening if the listener has not been drawn into a relationship — a mutual emotional acknowledgment of shared interests — with the speaker.

We communicate essentially to increase our well-being by connecting to our surroundings and having a beneficial influence on those around us, whether at the physical, emotional, mental or spiritual level.

We communicate to relieve ourselves of isolation and fear, by finding our common connection with others.

If we try to communicate with those who won't hear, we will not feel relieved or in any greater connection with our surroundings.

But if we communicate genuinely with those who want to hear, we will feel relieved and connected.

So for any communication, we need to establish a relationship by sharing on the feeling level. Just a "Good morning" or "I'm looking forward to this time together" will do wonders for opening another's mind to our message.

Too often we think that expressing feelings is a favor to the other guy — letting him or her know how we feel so that they can adjust themselves accordingly. But emotional expression is essentially for us.

When we have expressed an emotion, it almost invariably changes in intensity or nature. It loses its power to control us. Carl Jung said that true communication transforms both the listener and the speaker.

If we are stuck in the manipulative stage, we need above all to dare to feel again and to share our emotions.

Courtesy

Courtesy with those closest to us is the mechanism by which we take the time to share on the feeling level and to acknowledge our commonality.

A child's emotions are every bit as complex as any adult's and far more complex than many adults imagine their own emotions to be.

Greetings, expressing gratitude, waiting patiently for a response to our message, quiet listening, avoiding interrupting, respecting physical space and possessions and making requests graciously with no thought of reward or consequence, are the tools for replacing manipulation with genuine communication.

Controlling The Uncontrollable

We use manipulation essentially as a way to avoid or impose control. We quit manipulative behaviors most easily by becoming assertive in setting our personal boundaries within which we are in control and by accepting the limits of our control over others.

When we try to bolster our self-esteem by exerting power over others through manipulation, instead of by connecting through communication, we find ourselves more alone than ever. We cannot respect someone we can manipulate. Without respect, we never feel we are dealing with equals. The loneliness increases relentlessly — the more successful we are, the more overpowering it becomes. Without that special human activity of relating, connecting and sharing our humanness with others, our self-esteem continues to dwindle, no matter how much power over others we have amassed.

As parents we are faced with an emptiness that seems to set us apart from others, who seem to just enjoy and feel comfortable with their kids. We try to manipulate for parental respect, filial affection, achievement and so forth, but we cannot escape the hollow feeling. When we sense a hollowness in our children, the pain can become acute.

As parents we may seek in our children the ultimate confirmation that our skeptical view of life is accurate, that each is out for himself, and that happiness comes from power over others. Thankfully our children will not give us this confirmation.

We need to accept that we do not control the life of our children. We can only love them, protect them from risks beyond their capability to appreciate, guide them with empathy and example and enjoy them. But this is enough.

At the same time that we respect their boundaries, we can find our own. We can reclaim our right to feel tired, angry, disappointed, proud, silly, monstrous, confused or elated, and to communicate these feelings.

By communicating our boundaries, our personhood, our importance to ourselves, we grow in self-esteem and begin to feel in control of our own contentment. Then we may feel more and more the need to express elation, joy, love, peace, fun and serenity.

You may have heard as a child that feelings hurt others, that your anger or thoughtlessness caused someone's depression or drinking, that your feelings are powerful and dangerous. But they are not, so long as you are willing to communicate them in ways that make clear that they are your own legitimate possession. No one else is responsible for them.

By doing this we acknowledge our feelings and free them to go. We validate ourselves and give ourselves the courage to drop old attitudes and behaviors, no matter how ingrained. We reinforce the ones that make us feel good about ourselves.

We also validate the person with whom we share our feelings by showing that we trust them with our humanness. Children respond extremely well to our demonstration of this kind of trust, once they have become convinced by experience that there are no strings attached.

Communication Tips

We need to practice real listening and to learn to respond with empathy instead of with advice and judgment. Empathy can be learned.

Here are some ways to instantly improve communication and empathy, the great validator with kids.

1. **Use the name**. Use the child's name with positive statements, and often.
2. **Give "I" messages**. Use, "I feel . . . (feeling word), because you . . . (non-threatening description of recent action)." We need to cultivate the art of constructive confrontation, with "I" messages instead of "you" messages.
3. **Give eye contact**. Look into the child's eyes and see not what but who is in there — usually a most lovable human being.
4. **Reflect feelings**. If faced with angry words or deeds or interpersonal confusion, try to label the feelings and then let the child correct you if the label is wrong. For example:

    Parent: "You are very angry because I said no."

    Child: "I'm not angry, I'm furious because you do this all the time."

    Parent: "You're furious because you think I keep saying no to you."

    Child: "Yes." The sigh of relief from getting heard is often audible. From here solutions can be found together. In addition, you help give your child a vocabulary for feelings.
5. **Respect comfort zone**. Be quick to recognize changes in your state of mind and tell your child about it. "It makes me uncomfortable when you yell so loud (curse at your sister, refuse to do a chore you have already agreed to, resist doing

your homework before dinner, talk in a sassy tone on the phone, etc.)."

We need to agree to disagree, recognizing the unique expression of humanity that each of us is.

Notice when others' comfort zones are shifting and articulate it if possible.

6. **Listen.** You don't always have to respond, answer or begin conversation. Try to listen and hear. Listening to silence can be constructive when it gives the child time to collect his thoughts and believe he will be heard when he speaks. Don't read something into silence. If it makes you uneasy, say merely, "This silence makes me uneasy. Will you share your thoughts with me or shall we wait until later?"

7. **Maintain linguistic integrity.** Try to say what you mean and mean what you say. Know your likes and your wants and communicate them. If you get what you ask for and it doesn't feel good, change your requests. Let your words reflect your unfolding self-awareness.

8. **Fend off manipulation with kindness.** It is perfectly okay to say, "I feel manipulated here." But not, "You are manipulating me." If you are the parent, you are in control of whether you are manipulated or not.

Feelings are yours. Don't cast blame on your child for trying to manipulate or for making you feel manipulated, whether or not they are doing it. Rather, focus attention on candor about your feelings. A person who knows herself and is not afraid to express her deepest self cannot be manipulated.

If we speak genuinely, there is no pay-off for the manipulative effort and the child will soon learn to forgo it.

9. **Put time on your side.** If tempers flare, set a date to discuss the issue or the way you handle issues, or both, best done at different times if possible. Avoid urgent attempts at resolution. Urgency destroys any sense of priorities, proportion and perspective.

Instead use patience, postponement and creative procrastination. You will have a much greater chance of a successful outcome. Less than a tenth of what we think is urgent is truly urgent. The rest will benefit by being put off to a predetermined time.

Do carry through with the appointed discussion when the time comes.

When we let others follow their own inclinations in little things, we begin to discover that they are more willing than we had imagined to help us, to cooperate with us and to love us. We begin to imagine a life free of manipulation and filled with affirmative communication.

Our parents manipulated because of a life-threatening dependency. We are manipulating without any such excuse. It is not hard to lose all self-respect. We will soon stop being surprised that our children don't respect us if we stay stuck in the manipulative stage. But with the challenges they bring to our lives, we may get the impetus to change.

Otherwise we may settle into despair.

From Despair To Trust   12

In the stage of despair, the last bastion of hope is gone. The adult child's self-esteem reaches bottom. She has abandoned her inherent human rights one by one: her right to feel as she wishes, her right to act free of others' judgments, her right to think independently, and now her right to believe in herself.

She has in effect acted out completely the emotional abandonment she felt as a child in her co-dependent home.

The stage of despair traps you if your most impressionable years for relationship training occurred when your alcoholic family was completely nonfunctional in meeting all but your most basic survival needs.

It also can occur when you have found life too empty as a result of the ultimate failure of defenses and manipulation to sustain any sense of purpose or self-worth.

Your Image Of Despair

We hear of children born into despair, who never taste a nourishing meal served on time or on clean plates, never hear a tender bedtime story, never see an after-school smile, never feel a casual parental hug, never smell a clean, fresh bed.

Such children tend to lack all energy and motivation and most easily and early fall into escapism, violence and addiction, often in their parents' footsteps.

Their highest motivation is survival and some sense of belonging, no matter how artificial. But even these hold no great value to them. Minimizing pain is their driving force. Having abandoned long ago any normal expectation of pleasure, love or happiness, they seek to feel alive only through the temporary exhilaration of fear or even self-loathing.

But even these children have the spark of spiritual self-worth still within, waiting for the opportunity to give light. Ministries such as Covenant House and Voyage House, two shelters for runaways in New York City and other cities, have demonstrated repeatedly that the most hardened youth has a good chance of revising his world view and regenerating his self-esteem if he is exposed to nonjudgmental, unconditional love together with the basic necessities of healthy living — namely, food, shelter, clothing and meaningful nonthreatening human contact.

It is not just kids born in the streets who face despair. Just as the picture of the wino on skid row for decades prevented middle-class families from admitting they had alcohol problems, so the picture of the desperate young thug in the street can prevent us from coming to grips with the fact that a person can sit in a nice house with a full refrigerator and a full bank account, with two identifiable parents both alive, and still be in absolute spiritual, life-threatening despair.

In recovery groups, people speak of hitting bottom. All feeling humans have desperate moments when hope seems to leave us and we feel totally alone. But it is the frequency of these moments and what we do with them that matters. Hitting bottom can be the beginning of recovery, and it is our decision alone.

Anger And Rage

If you are in the stage of despair as a parent, you are dangerous to the life and health of your children as well as to yourself. The latent anger of adult children is ferocious and can make your child feel confused and insecure, even when you think you are hiding it well. Those closest and most vulnerable — your children — are the most likely victims of your negative outbursts.

Rage might be characterized as anger which has detached itself from any particular event, person, place or thing. It lies in wait for any provocation to explode its full force on whoever is near.

The rage of co-dependency has a life of its own and can be passed on indefinitely until someone consciously chooses to change. All love is stifled by our rage.

The sight of our own child in pain or rage can throw us into deeper despair and self-hatred, possibly leading to violence and abuse against child or self. Wasting and battering are common in families where an adult child raising children is holding on to old ways of expressing despair, bursting with rage and still trapped in the limited options of a young child.

It is in this area that our newspaper headlines are so heart-rending. For every case of child abuse and criminal charges, there is a family in the stage of despair. They need a great deal more than the blame of society dropped on their heads.

The frequency and intensity of despair may be increased by this constant media exposure to others in its clutches. Can we look forward to a time when coupled with each article describing desperate anti-family behavior, there will be an article about someone who turned their despair into an opportunity for recovery? With headlines just as big and with accessible phone numbers?

Signs Of Despair

It is harder to recognize despair in a home where we fill a parental role than in almost any other circumstance. We have the accoutrements of success — a house, an income, children. We often put off finding help because we use these exterior indicia to reassure ourselves — manipulating our feelings still — that we don't have to do anything yet. "We aren't desperate."

But we may well be, and our family may suffer needlessly if we will not acknowledge it.

Here are the major signs of despair:

1. **Loss of energy.** Everything seems like just a bit too much effort. You ask your three-year-old to get her own dinner. You forget to take your nine-year-old to his game practice. You don't get up in the morning and you see your children taking on burdens you swore no child of yours would ever have to take on.

2. **Loss of concentration.** You forget why you are doing something and don't carry through on tasks. Your children remind you often of your plans and commitments.

3. **Trouble making decisions.** The pros and cons of daily decisions seem overwhelming. You worry about what each person will think and decide there is no harmonious way to act and it doesn't matter anyhow.

4. **Loss of interest**. Old hobbies and concerns seem petty and boring now.
5. **Numbness to feeling**. The old manipulative games and arguments leave you numb. You aren't up for a good fight anymore, even with the old provocations.
6. **Your child stops asking**. Your child seems suddenly more independent, no longer asking for your help, advice, approval, attention or any interaction at all.
7. **Your health deteriorates**. Friends tell you that you don't look well. You increase your smoking, drinking, snacking, medications, late nights and so forth. You venture outside or away from home less often or else seldom come home.
8. **Pessimism**. You lose your sense of outrage or righteous anger. You lose all trust in others. All seems equally vacuous and hopeless.

Holding On And Letting Go

If we are stuck in the despair stage of co-dependency, our greatest sensitivity with our children will be in the area of trust and maturity. They may be our last remaining sign that we are still in control. We fear losing them and we resent their growing independence. They sense our dependence on them and begin to dislike themselves for thinking of abandoning us.

If we retard their independence by our desperate dependency, we can also drive them away faster, long before they are ready.

Children's emerging maturity can also make us jealous. We see them at the beginning of their lives when we, in despair, think we are at the end of ours.

If you find yourself clinging to your child no matter what her age, unwilling to see any progress toward independence and constantly saying things like, "Here, let me do that for you," or, "I'll take care of it, you go play," or, "Don't ever leave me," then you may be in a state of quiet desperation.

Even if we have lost them already — they have moved out, gone to an estranged spouse or otherwise shut off connections — there are always new ways to share ourselves once we discover we have something within us to share.

Our first job is to discover that unique value we each have just by being ourselves and by being somebody's parent.

Rebirth

If you see that you are stuck in the stage of despair, you have the power to take it as an opportunity to start again. You can break despair's grip by first reaching out just a little each day, to things, creatures and people you know you can trust.

Start with a flower perhaps, a thunderstorm, a painting, a photo, and then gradually work up to a pet. When comfortable with the unconditional love of even a fish, a dog or a cat, move on to a person who you know could have no angle.

Gradually, you will learn to trust yourself, to listen attentively and to speak honestly with yourself.

Finally you will learn to trust some larger force outside yourself that is responsible for the goodness that is starting to be evident in your life, as the invisible connectedness between you and those around you begins to manifest in your life.

Rebuilding trust is a most difficult task. Each slip seems to be proof that the trust was undeserved or misplaced. Children, too, like anyone else, will be suspicious of newly placed trust. Be patient, with yourself and them, as you change your ways. Enthusiasm for life will be reborn.

First Tools For Ending Despair

Once we have made a decision to look for a change, there is no treatment so successful as finding a group of people with the same problem, who work to heal themselves by practicing trusting each other, if only just to listen nonjudgmentally.

Another tool is to imagine what we would feel in a particular situation if we hadn't given up all caring and then express that feeling and try to own it. We can get our feelings back. This is called *acting as if* or "fake it 'til you make it." It will nurture that spark of spiritual life within each parent like a warm breeze on a candle.

If we can open the door but a crack, our children will come forward before long to pass through.

Full Circle

Often we are afraid of more intimacy with our children. We want them at a certain distance, no farther away but no closer.

We want them to think we are who we wish we had been and we
fear abandonment and rejection if they were to get close enough to
see who we really are. We fear from our children the same abandonment and rejection we once felt from our parents.

We've come full circle.

Secrets

Secrets are the great plague of adult children. We feel that if the
truth were known, we would be patently unlovable. Suzanne Somers
described in her autobiographical book, *Keeping Secrets,* the incredible burden of trying to fool all the people all the time. It gets
hopelessly tiresome. Abraham Lincoln said it couldn't be done. And
it leads to despair.

Psychologist Pauline Rose Clance describes in her book, *The
Impostor Syndrome,* the nagging feeling that no matter how well you
appear to have done, you are hiding the worthlessness of what you
really are. Charles Hobbs described this feeling as giving up being
human "beings" and valuing ourselves only as "human doings."

Hans Seyle, world-renowned expert on stress, says that stress per
se is neither healthy nor unhealthy. Life is a process of responding
and adjusting to changing conditions. Without stress we die. It is the
divergence between our inner values and our outer lives that causes
negative stress.

If we believe we have no inner value and are determined to hide
our desperation, we will be faced as parents with a child who wants
to love us and who wants our love. One of the best things we can
do is learn to trust the child.

Trust The Little Child

We need to trust our children when they reflect back our spiritual
value. If our children see something in us, it is there. Believe them. In
the Judeo-Christian and other traditions, a little child will lead the way.

If your children cry, scream or send nasty letters, they still see
something they care about and want to connect with. If they see it,
it is there.

Even if they see nothing and have given up on you and you wish
they hadn't, that wish is something of value. You can start with that
wish and build on that to pull yourself out of despair.

You can use prayer effectively — religious or meditative — to
put your heart and soul into that wish and begin to see that your

energy, your concentration, your interest, your feelings, your spiritual health and your love of life can all be reclaimed with the spark of love for a child.

At the heart of moving into recovery is our acceptance that we ourselves were worth parenting. We cannot live wholly in the present as parents unless we truly believe we have had our turn to be children. If our parents were unable to parent us adequately, we must let go of those many protective mechanisms that helped save us from that realization as children but ate away at us as adults.

The experience of having our own children is a unique gift that allows us to see firsthand that children are worth parenting. If we let ourselves appreciate this truth, that we were just as helpless, lovable, funny, cute, engaging, feisty and irresistible as our own children are, we can move into accepting the reality that we were worth parenting.

If there is blame, we must move it out of ourselves and place it squarely on the shoulders of the multi-factorial family-crippling disease of addiction and the patterns of co-dependency it generates. Then we must move into forgiveness for ourselves and all those we've blamed along the way before we came to this knowledge.

Finally, we can rebuild our self-esteem from within. We can reparent ourselves, heal the child within, care for the inner child. Whatever its name, to be successful, this process of moving beyond the stages of co-dependency into recovery and independence requires a special willingness to heal.

Elements Of Willingness

We need not be perfect to break out of co-dependency and create a healthy life for our family. We need only to be willing to change in these ways:

1. **A willingness to believe** we are inherently valuable just as human beings. Experience of millions of people recovering from co-dependency has demonstrated that this willingness is ultimately inseparable from a willingness to believe that there is some overarching unity, some essential goodness or purpose, some higher power in the universe or some innate higher self that gives us a place and a value and a direction as individuals, despite our inability to know and understand the big picture.

2. **A willingness to risk change** in interpersonal relationships by replacing old habits of rejection, defenses and manipulation with honest sharing of ourselves.

3. **A willingness to confront** our feelings, letting them rise, feeling them, digging behind them again and again, examining each one with its associated thoughts, until we hit the rock bottom good feelings that ultimately motivate everything we do.

4. **A willingness to give our time** and attention to our relationship with our children.

5. **A willingness to wait,** to stop and think before we speak or act.

6. **A willingness to trust** in the parent-child bond as the bedrock for our link with our child, a bond that has worked well for millions of years, a bond that is uniquely human in its power to heal and help us grow, and a bond that will survive the destruction of chemical intrusion into our childhood home, no matter how late we think it is to begin our recovery with our child.

Tori

Tori was frustrated with her daughter's fidgeting. In recovery for a while, she resisted blaming the child and let herself feel her own frustration. Then she traced it back as follows, alternating between feelings and associated thoughts.

First she remembered her parents' frustration at her own fidgeting and her fear and spite at them. Then came their anger and loud words and her pain and self-rebuke at causing them distress. Then it was their helplessness and her confusion and pity for them. Then came their imperfection and her surprise and compassion. Then she noticed their attempts to have her believe in them and her appreciation for the effort and love it showed. Then she acknowledged their failure and her frustration and disappointment. Finally she saw her own righteousness and felt a renewed love for herself.

This may seem like a long tortured process, but with a little practice it can be done in a matter of 15 seconds. At the bottom of this introspection through feelings, Tori found a frightened confused child who wanted to please and couldn't, and who found an outlet for her frustration relatively safely by fidgeting.

Now she could forgive her parents for making her feel so inadequate about her chosen outlet for childhood anxiety. And she could let go of her hang-up about her own child's fidgeting by either tolerating it, now that she had removed the pain it restimulated, or by communicating openly with her child about it free of anxieties, reactions and negative attitudes from the past.

In either case, she felt good enough about herself and her unblocked relationship with her child that she didn't really care whether she fidgeted or not. She discovered it just wasn't that important.

In the end, the habit disappeared on its own. Whether it was lowered family anxiety or just a stress the child had worked through for herself, we can never know. But Tori got her baggage out of the way, so that the child could move on at her own rate for her own inner reasons. Tori found it most gratifying.

Something as small and common as fidgeting can be the trigger for a major outburst of despair, wounding those we love and increasing our shame. With recovery, one small step at a time, we feel the joys of rebirth into a world that cares.

Your Recovery And Your Child | 13

The best gift you can give your child is the gift of your recovery. It is the gift of knowledge of how to change a life for the better.

In the recovery stage, you move from the reaction habits of the other stages into a new mental state of free choice and conscious focus on the present in all you do.

You rebuild your self-esteem and unlearn the mistaken lesson of your own unworthiness.

You stop assuming that your feelings and needs go unheeded. You learn new ways of relating to people without defenses and manipulative games.

You learn to dream big dreams and to work on small, manageable tasks to achieve those dreams.

You let go of any guilt over imperfections in your parenting of the past and focus your attention on being clear with your child now, about your feelings, motives and goals.

You learn not to fight the bad times but just to let them pass, as you prepare yourself to enjoy the good times. You find that inward peace brings outward peace.

Contacting Spiritual Reality

In her book, *Daily Affirmations*, Rokelle Lerner says, "My happiness depends on how clearly I see the spiritual reality behind all appearances."

Our success in beginning or progressing in our recovery as adult
children raising children depends upon our recognizing the spiritual
reality of our children and of our bond to them behind the everyday
chores and challenges of parenting.

In my book, *You Can Postpone Anything But Love*, I explored the
spiritual essence of the parent-child bond and the way that we can
build on it in even the most mundane situations. If we stay in
contact with this basic truth, we can turn even conflicts and crises
into validating experiences that leave parent and child renewed in
individual self-esteem and mutual trust.

As we have seen, the adult child is haunted by a spiritual gap.
When we accept and build on the spiritual essence of the parent-
child bond, we enlist our parenting experience as a learning ground
for our emerging spirituality.

By now I hope you have been able to identify your most typical
cluster of reactions in parenting by considering the stages of co-
dependency, your sibling birth order and your key sensitivity areas.

Whenever you find yourself engaging in one of those reactions or
having *déjà vu* when you see your child's response to you, the first
thing you must do is defuse the explosive energy of the moment by
taking the time to think.

Urgency

Thomas Jefferson recommended counting to 10. Just remember-
ing to count at all can bring us back to some sense of proportion in
the situation. In parenting our sense of urgency often becomes
paramount. We rationalize that we want to appear decisive, to have
clear rules, to be consistent or to be spontaneous with our children.

But, said with tender loving care, these are only rationalizations.
They hide from us, for the moment, the pervading sense of urgency
that we have brought with us within ourselves to the situation. None
of these ideas carries any real value, because the truth is that our
child is a spiritual being and senses the essence of our state of
mind. We cannot deceive her into thinking that when we blurt out
half-baked conclusions, yell, curse or hurl angry words to cover up
insecurity or anxiety, we are really exhibiting decisiveness, clarity,
consistency or spontaneity.

Instead we do better to assume that our children can read our
every feeling. They cannot read our minds, remember. They cannot
know where our anxiety comes from and will assume it is them. But

they can read anxiety in our faces and body language. They may well misinterpret the underlying thought if we have not been genuine with them about it but they will not miss the feeling.

If this transparency of parents — "She sees right through me" — is scary, how much more scary is it to hide from your child so long and intently that eventually she doesn't see you at all? Some adult children have had the painful experience of having their child shut them off, give them a double dose of their own distancing medicine and reject and abandon them, just as they most feared their parents would do.

To begin our recovery, we must set aside this urgency and give ourselves the time to think. Next we must know who it is we are dealing with.

Spiritual Equality

Communication is a two-way street. Even with very small children, true communication does not take place unless it is between equals — spiritual equals. I have talked to hundreds of parents who complained that their children did not share their feelings, triumphs or failures with them, even though they felt strongly that they could have and would have been helpful to their children.

But time and time again, I have found that the parent was sharing virtually none of her feelings, triumphs or failures with the child. There are two serious results. First, the child has no model for sharing. Perhaps grown-ups don't share, he will deduce. Second, he misses the sense of mutual trust that comes from both parties sharing themselves.

These parents report almost universally that they avoid discussing finances, war, sexual matters, gossip, family plans, politics, crime and their work, thinking these things will variously bore, confuse or distort the thinking of their children. And usually, they do not share their feelings either because they are either unaware of them or think they are unimportant compared to the importance of "raising the children."

By eliminating feelings from our parental sharing, we have indeed made it impossible to talk about any topic without boring, confusing and distorting. Of course our children will not benefit from sharing details of these matters. But sharing our feelings about them is sharing ourselves.

You might say, "I'm feeling really wonderful after all the praise I got from my supervisor (neighbor, doctor, etc.)."

Or, "I'm feeling sorry about a good friend whose daughter is going through a nasty divorce."

These feelings validate our children as respected, trusted beings and model for them the communication we so want to get back from them.

When we interact as equals, we should not ignore that we have superior age, size, experience, knowledge and skills but on the spiritual level — of love, respect, connectedness — we are equals. The child is just as spiritually independent as we are, as responsible for his own destiny, as deserving of respect and trust, as capable of giving and receiving love, as worthy of a full and happy life, as any adult.

We will not be able to know or learn our children's thoughts or feelings if we do not share ours. And the spiritual equality works both ways. If we need to avoid feeling superior, we must also avoid feeling inferior. If we do, we must find our way back to equality just as emphatically as if we feel superior.

Many an adult child raising children is in the position of trying to be superior in order to hide her feeling of inferiority to her child.

If we find ourselves in the grip of uncomfortable behavior or feelings, we need to stop and think. We need to remind ourselves that our child will never lose anything by our taking a few moments to collect ourselves, to integrate, unify and orient ourselves to the truth of our basic spiritual connectedness and equality.

Recovery Of What? From What?

In the medical context, recovery refers to recovery of health, from disease. Webster's dictionary defines "to recover" as, "to regain after losing; restore, as oneself, from sickness, faintness, or the like; retrieve, make up for, reclaim for use, as resources or materials; rescue; regain a former state or condition as after misfortune or disturbance of mind."

All of these definitions hold true in the context of adult children in recovery while raising children. Adult children need to regain and restore self-esteem.

They need to reclaim and retrieve the full spectrum of feelings and options with which they were born, after having lost them through no fault of their own.

They need to rescue themselves from unresolved pain and loss and regain their former state of spiritual wholeness and connectedness after misfortune and disturbance of mind.

No wonder "recovery" is such a popular word for what we are seeking in our escape from co-dependency!

It is a basic tenet of the many recovery programs that use the 12 Steps to spiritual recovery that to help others we must be selfish. We must meet our needs and indulge our highest goals if we want to have the strength, courage and wisdom to help someone else.

Both Albert Schweitzer and Mother Teresa, probably the most well-known and admired examples in the world of true altruism and dedication to helping others, have specifically articulated that they take good care of themselves in order to be of service, and that they help others for their own personal satisfaction in the work.

Total health of mind, body and spirit is not a steady state achieved once and then maintained by controlling outside forces into the future. Instead it is an unfolding, an ongoing process, a becoming that must be in motion to offer its benefits to those close to us and to the universe at large.

Recovery isolated from the ongoing process of raising our children is ultimately no recovery at all. Like an addict who has no trouble staying dry in a recovery unit but must learn new ways to think and act once returned to the normal world, so our recovery cannot stay isolated from the relationships that matter to us most.

We can trust the spiritual reality of the parent-child bond to create positive changes in our relationship as we recover. Sooner or later even what appear to be basic traits that disturb us in our child will adjust to the improved environment.

Values, Goals And Self-Esteem In Recovery

Sometimes we don't realize that we can nurture our own self-esteem. The most direct way to build self-esteem is to discover your highest personal values, establish realistic goals in line with these and then accomplish those goals. Taking action based on your highest goals exposes you to experiences that show you your inherent value and build self-esteem.

Sharing our recovery process with our children by improving our responses to them is among the most self-affirming things an adult child raising children can do to rebuild self-esteem.

What kind of values and goals can we set in our recovery?

Many of us have a series of reactive personal values — like, *I won't be irrational, inconsistent, angry, violent or pushy.* These are reactions to our own dysfunctional family.

In recovery we need a series of positive values to crowd out the temptation of old habits and models. We need to define ourselves not as negatives — "I won't be like my parents" or "I'm okay as long as I don't do that!" — but as positives. Examples might be showing affection, inspiring excellence, modeling life-long learning and growth, trusting in the spiritual goodness of people, minding my own business, respecting the boundaries of others, defenselessness, projecting hope and faith.

Any series of values that touches your highest image of yourself as a parent will lead you in this process to practical goals that will become attainable.

For example, if you hold as a value the creating of an atmosphere of familial affection, implementing goals might be:

1. Giving your child direct eye contact for at least 30 seconds on two different occasions each day.
2. Having a chat with your child about what signs of affection you each like best.
3. Visualizing each morning a warm response from your teenager.
4. Doing one fun, silly thing together each week, like miniature golf, dominoes, taking a walk, dress-up, watching a favorite video, and watching it again!

When any of these goals is accomplished, you will have a big and lasting boost to your self-esteem.

As self-esteem gradually improves, goals become easier to set and easier to attain. We begin to appreciate the power we have over the way we feel each day. We discover that our positive values are more a part of the real us than any number of habitual thoughts or behaviors that we may have used in the past to define ourselves and were therefore fearful to give up.

We begin to discover our real selves as powerful, lovable, spiritual beings.

Spiritual Freedom

Management trainer Charles Hobbs has listed five levels of freedom and responsibility in relationships between a supervisor and someone supervised, whether it be employee, student or child. These are, from least freedom and responsibility to most of each, as follows:

1. You wait to be told what to do.
2. You ask what to do.
3. You meet your supervisor's expectations.
4. You discover what to do and get approval to proceed.
5. You go about your business with periodic reporting.

Most adult children are stuck at one of the first three levels. We are busy trying to figure out what we are supposed to do, either by waiting to hear, or by trying to figure out others' expectations, or by tentatively asking, hopefully without bringing down extra demands or criticism upon ourselves. We don't even imagine any greater freedom than that.

We would feel uncomfortable and fearful if left to go about our business with unlimited trust and only periodic reporting. Even the mild initiative of finding out what to do and seeking prior approval has too often invited criticism, blame and recrimination.

Yet full self-determination, with freedom and responsibility to the fullest, is just what is expected of an adult, especially a parent. As parents and heads of households, we are automatically in the position of having no one to tell us what to do or to give us advance approval to protect us from hindsight and Monday morning quarterbacking. There is no one who has a supervisory responsibility over our parenting.

We may not let this stop us. We may go about inventing one. We may try to push the supervisory role onto a parent, doctor, counselor, spouse, TV personality or other but the responsibility stays with us and advice-shopping ultimately brings us no relief. We may live in constant fear of the freedom we have as parents.

Instead, we must rise to the occasion by finding the resources within ourselves to discover on our own what must be done and to do it, with periodic review in light of our progress and our highest personal values.

In recovery we are seeking independence, freedom and responsibility, no matter how scary it may be at first. It will help us accept our freedom if we focus on the positive and build our expectations not on what might go wrong, but on what might go right.

Expectations And Self-Fulfilling Prophecy

Our parental expectations act as a self-fulfilling prophecy for our children. By creating a positive vision of our decisions, communications and interactions, we maximize our spiritual influence toward our desired result. We counteract what may be years of unintentional projections of negative expectations which tended to create anxiety and mistakes in the child.

If we dwell on worries and fretting, our preoccupation and lack of trust make it likely that whatever might go wrong will.

On the other hand, if we are relaxed, attentive and confident, without judging or testing, our children are most likely to behave in ways that make us feel proud.

It is essential that we learn to visualize our goals as being accomplished on the spiritual level first. We must visualize our child exhibiting his true goodness and ability, for example, instead of visualizing an "A" on his test.

In our vision of our child, it is helpful to distinguish between trust and faith. Trust can be proven misplaced. Faith cannot. Faith is only justified on the spiritual level and cannot be proven wrong. Faith in our children can never be shown to be misplaced. We may trust them with a job beyond their capabilities or judgment and be proven mistaken. But our faith in their spiritual goodness and basic will to live in accordance with that goodness can never be shown to be wrong or even dangerous, no matter how untrustworthy they may seem in any specific instance.

We show our faith by minding our own business, accepting mistakes and giving the child as much freedom as he can handle. Using the five-step progression towards freedom and responsibility for our children in the same manner we used it for ourselves, we might at first assume that the child starts at level one. But this is not the case. As parents, we need to decide which areas of the child's life can accommodate how much freedom.

From birth, some areas are already at the fifth level. A child's spiritual connection with the universe and the realm of his feelings and thoughts are his alone. Periodic review is the very most you can hope for and even that you cannot count on or insist upon. You get it only when you have earned his trust. But remember, you never lose his faith so if you do not have his trust, you can regain it.

The area of perceptions and interpretations will tend to be at the fourth level in a healthy family environment. Typically the child makes independent discoveries through play and experience and seeks parental approval of lessons learned.

If you have been in patterns of manipulation or defenses, your children will be as reluctant to ask permission and seek prior approval as you were as a child. They may even be reluctant to make suggestions or even ask what must be done. They may just wait for someone to tell them what to think and what to do. A mind is a terrible thing to waste.

In recovery, you can work with your children to free their perceptions and experimentation from the tight grip of your expectations. And you can use positive reinforcement to increase their learning capacity, so that they learn to trust their perceptions and play with them to test them out.

In many areas of childhood behavior, meeting the expectations you set as a parent by word and example is the level of freedom most appropriate for your children. Examples are table manners, working with dangerous tools, learning sports, hygiene routines, sleep routines. Luckily, children are quick to recognize that they do not want any more freedom than this in these areas, so long as you are quick to give them freedom in the areas where it is appropriate.

If our children persist in asking us what to do, say or think or if they always wait to be told what to do, then we should take it as a sign that they need more responsibility delegated to them. If they do not steadily seek more freedom, then chances are they are stuck in a rut of low self-esteem and need positive parental validation.

One of the greatest rewards of recovery is to discover that everything we do to recover sets a valuable model for our children and helps to validate them as well as ourselves. Little things we do like stopping to think, may be far more important lessons in positive, mature behavior than all the homework in the world or whatever else we feel determined to get them to learn.

Just by taking the little steps each day to allow ourselves room to recover, we are sharing recovery with our children. As we work on ourselves, we will begin to notice positive changes in our interactions. Beginning with taking a moment to think, here are some tools we can use.

Tools For Sharing Recovery

1. Take a moment to **think**, letting your sense of urgency melt away for the time being.
2. **Choose words carefully,** that neither patronize your child nor set her on a pedestal. Neither condescend nor try to impress.
3. Take and give time each day, 20 minutes to an hour depending on the child's age (the shorter time for the younger child), specifically for **each to be alone,** deciding together ahead of time when it shall be and for the younger child, what they might do during that time.

4. Take and give time each day, 20 minutes to an hour (the shorter time for the older child), specifically for parent and child **to be together**, deciding together ahead of time who will have say over how the time is spent (alternating weeks is one possibility).

5. Arrange **meetings** to discuss these plans and any troublesome issues, deciding together ahead of time when and where to meet.

6. Have a meeting once a week when good and bad things about your interactions are aired in a **reaction-free zone**. That is a time in which each listens only, agreeing not to draw any presumptions or conclusions nor to ask any probing questions under the guise of "just want to understand," but only to listen. Both must share, in order to maintain the mutual vulnerability as a deterrent to using the complaints as weapons later.

7. Decide **before answering a question** whether it is possible for you to answer it, and don't be afraid to say it's impossible right now, if it is. For example, you may need more knowledge, thinking, inspiration. Or the question may ask for an opinion about what's right for someone else, a question you cannot answer except by imagining what you might be inclined to do were you faced with the same situation, which, you must remember, you are not. Kids are quick to ask, "Should I?" But make your answer slow and consistent with your new awareness, in recovery, of the limits of your knowledge of and control over others. Practice any of these answer options that feel unfamiliar to you so that they will be available when appropriate:

   - "I don't know."
   - "That is beyond my knowledge or control."
   - "I am not ready to decide that right now. I will get back to you tomorrow on that."
   - "How can I help you find the answer to that one?"
   - "That's impossible for me right now."
   - "I would like to help you if you would like."
   - "How can I help you make up your mind on that?"

8. When a child brings you a problem, **ask for suggested solutions** or options and ask how you can help him choose and implement one. Guide his thought process rather than imposing your thoughts, no matter how hard he may press you.

9. Speak for yourself. Use **"I" messages** to express feelings and requests, instead of judgments, predictions, commands, threats or rationalizations.

10. **Let go of grim determination** whenever you feel it.

11. Make **mutual decisions about responsibilities** within the family and have periodic reviews and revisions, keeping in mind age-appropriateness and time and priority constraints of both parent and child.

12. As much as possible **leave decisions to the youngest** person with the necessary information and maturity to handle it. This builds the child's sense of mastery, develops parental confidence in the child's mastery and increases the child's trust that his freedom will expand as he is capable.

13. Discuss and predetermine any **reward system** you intend to use. This way you can avoid a dangerous cluster of rationalizations about reinforcement theories. Sometimes we want to believe we are using positive and negative reinforcement consistent with good training theory, when in fact we may be venting ancient clogged emotions that are wholly inappropriate and disproportionate to the situation.

14. Articulate and explore together personal **boundaries and comfort zones**. These will change with the age of the child, with the progression of our recovery and with any related processes the child undergoes simultaneously.

15. Develop **joyful times** together that will help crowd out the stressful times.

16. When making a decision affecting the child, **ask for her input**, making it clear ahead of time that it will not decide the case if it will not, but that you will take it into consideration and let her know your countervailing reasons if you decide against her wishes.

17. Find out what each of you finds most funny and share it — like joke books, comedy videos, greeting cards, etc. Use the healing power of **laughter** together regularly.

Change

In recovery we come to accept the state of continuous change that childhood represents. Change is always unsettling and for adult children of dysfunctional families it is downright frightening. With little faith in themselves and long experience that if things change they get worse, not better, most adult children feel completely adapted out. They feel drained, unable to adjust one more degree, inflexible.

At some point change threatens to undo the bundle of reactions that have appeared to take care of our deepest wounds. We want to have things stay the same.

But one thing a parent can count on is that a child will never ever stay the same.

Recovery can be very confusing, stirring up long submerged stuff from way back when, sometimes shocking us with revelations about where our favorite reactions and parenting tools really come from. We may fear appearing even more ambivalent and inconsistent to our kids than before.

But children respond to the essence of things much more than we realize. Pop psychology says consistency is everything. It's important but pop psychology doesn't realize that you can ask for more. The transition to something better might be worth the temporary upheaval.

Predictable parents are nice to have for setting your own survival course but parents who are rebuilding their sense of personal value and a positive attitude toward life are worth a period of uncertainty and ambiguity. The child learns to share visions of really living, in joy and connectedness, not just survival. And she may get enough of a taste of recovery to have less fear than we did if she should ever need its comforts. She may even connect so well with our recovery that she will never suffer a spiritual gap at all.

Desensitizing The Key Sensitivity Areas

In contemplating your recovery and your children, examine each of the four key sensitivity areas and decide which decisions and activities in those areas need to be brought under more conscious direction.

I like to think of the sensitivity areas paired with the four realms of human activity to remind us of their all-inclusiveness. Love and affection relate to "I feel," the child's first conscious awareness.

Performance and mistakes relate to "I do," when the child learns about her physical relationship to the universe, to mother, to father, to objects, to her own body.

Learning and authority relate to "I think," as the child develops his imagination, reasoning, problem-solving and communication.

Trust and maturity relate to "I believe," that final uniquely human step of being consciously aware of consciousness, having a sense of value and purpose to your life.

If we bear in mind that our child has the God-given right to feel, do, think and believe as he or she chooses and that we have the same right, we can begin to share with each other our unique talents and gifts without imposing on the other's spiritual independence.

The next chapter presents some practical vignettes from everyday life to show you ways to share your recovery most effectively, so that your parenting will bring you and your child the satisfaction you want.

More Ways
To Share Recovery

14

Here are a few vignettes to illustrate for you how you might share your recovery-related thoughts with your children. Look them over and imagine how each might be adapted to situations in your family. Consider first the worst of times, when you are most under the influence of co-dependency, and consider second the best of times, when you are feeling strong in your recovery.

Use any of these as scripts to help stretch your recovery and feeling vocabulary. Rehearse or rewrite each in any way you want in line with your comfort zone.

By considering interactions before they happen and knowing what we want to say and how we can expect or hope to feel, we can make it more and more likely that the new words we like will prevail, even when the old bad messages or exaggerated emotions from the past threaten to take over.

Rewrite the scripts often, each time imagining how you would have reacted to the script when you were a child.

Sometimes we don't realize that as parents we are free to say exactly, word for word to our child what we would have liked most to hear from our own parents. Sometimes too, we don't realize that what we thought we wanted to hear back then may not have been what we really wanted. When we try an old wish fulfillment on our child, we may quickly find out that the solutions we dreamed of back then may not have been any better than what we got.

Today we are free to say what is right for us and our child now. Said Rokelle Lerner in *Daily Affirmations,* "My recovery is not dependent upon the resolution of yesterday's problems. Those problems are relevant only as they apply to today. My recovery takes place in the present."

Changing your way of interacting with your child is always a bit scary but your reading thus far should have given you a taste of the joy that awaits you and your child.

Minister Robert Schuller has said, "You can get anywhere from where you are."

Develop personal strategies to distract yourself from old emotions, like focusing on your child's eyes or hair, noticing the maturity evident in your own hands, looking up to the sky for inspiration: Anything that will give you a moment of time to step out of the past into the present.

Discover what in the current situation frustrates you. Perhaps like your parents, your children do not understand your needs as a person. Now consider whether children necessarily understand your needs. You never were taught the basic needs of a person as a child. Are you sure you know them now? You may have learned them only recently, the hard way. Now is your chance to teach your children the easy way.

Contrary to popular belief, children can learn very many things the easy way.

In reading these vignettes, imagine your own child in the listening role. Imagine a smile on your face as you say the words of the parent or something like them. Remember to keep your conversation light. If you are both alive and talking, nothing is so urgent that you cannot speak gently and hopefully.

Preteen Silence

When your preteen whines that you never see things his way, you might say, "You feel rejected because I don't see this thing your way."

He might answer with a grunt.

Then you might continue, "I want to see things from your point of view and would like to talk to you more openly about decisions I must make that affect you. Since you are growing up, there may be areas where I have not let you have enough say in these decisions.

"Please let me know when you think that is the case. I may still have to exercise parental dictatorship in areas I feel the risks are too great to give you a choice, but you can help me learn exactly how much you can handle by sharing more together."

Sibling Argument

When your two children are arguing endlessly, you might say, "I feel tense with so much noise and nasty words around. Please find a more peaceful way to resolve your problem.

"You have the right to disagree with each other. But in my environment there are some methods of resolving conflicts that are unacceptable to me. How can I help you discover a way to resolve this argument?"

Called To Be Judge

When your kids look to you to settle a dispute, you might say, "I am not in your shoes and can't tell what is right for the two of you. I believe you can find a solution between you. Let me know if you want help with suggestions but the decision is yours.

"Can I help you list all the factors you each care about in the situation? Maybe you will discover a solution from hearing out all your ideas."

Tantrums And Togetherness

Suppose your toddler insists fiendishly on one too many cookies, on staying too long at grandma's, on being too rough with the kitten, on mixing the salad with a shovel or on staying up too late at night.

If you are comfortable bending a little to compromise, you might say, "I know you want this very much because you enjoy it, it's fun and it's special. I'll let you do it now because you feel so strongly about it but I don't like your way of showing how strongly you feel.

"Next time, tell me how special it is to you and we can make it more pleasant for us both. I know you may have tried to tell me before but I am becoming a better listener. Another thing we can do is next time, let's decide together ahead of time how much, how long, or whatever."

Or if the behavior is unacceptable, you might say, "I can't let you do this now. I appreciate how much you want to do it and I want to spend a few minutes with you thinking up something else special we could do together that I am more comfortable with."

Teenage Rebellion

When your teenager ignores your advice about sleep hours, choice of friends, school priorities, too many video games, or self-

destructive habits like romantic pining, smoking, drinking, over-
or under-eating or sex, you might say, "I am very uncomfortable
with the choices you have been making recently in the area of
(whatever). . .

"You have a right to experiment with different lifestyles, compan-
ions and so on, but I hope you will consider the experience of
myself and others with this thing. I want very much to share my
experience with you."

And, "How about Tuesday nights we talk about what's going on
in our lives without judging, complaining or criticizing. Maybe just
better listening will help us understand each other better, without
playing games to see how much you can get away with or how
much I can tolerate. I'll start it off with my challenges of the week
and you don't have to go ahead unless you want to."

Or, "Your behavior is making me extremely uncomfortable and I
find it unacceptable in my home. We need to talk about what
behavior is acceptable in the house we share and what is not. As you
grow up I understand that you want more freedom to choose, and
I want to give it to you.

"I feel severely unappreciated when I have spent so much effort
on your health and well-being and see you now taking it so lightly.
You are a very important person to me and I am free to reject the
pain of watching you behave detrimentally to yourself or others.

"I feel confident of my parenting because I know I do not have
to tolerate behavior that I consider destructive to the health and
peace of my home and family. When shall we have a meeting about
this? You choose the date and time."

To Hug Or Not To Hug

If your 10-year-old gets stand-offish about affection, you might
say, "You're getting older now and have lots of different choices you
see in friends, on TV and elsewhere about affection. I feel great love
for you and want to express it in ways that you will feel comfortable
about and get the right message from.

"Would you rather I just hugged you instead of kissing you? Or
just squeezed your arm in front of friends instead of a hug? Could
we watch a video together just for fun on weekends? What would
you feel good about doing to let me know of your affection for me?
Could you give me your hand once in a while?

"What are your ideas on this?"

His Own Worst Critic

When a child is over-apologetic for a mistake, you might say, "You feel really bad about this. When I was little, I tried all the time to do things right. I had the impression that my parents expected me to be perfect.

"But now I'm learning, a little later than I'd like for you, that mistakes are natural. If you try to do something new you will often fail at first. And you wouldn't want never to try something new. You couldn't grow or learn that way.

"As a parent, sure, I like you to play it safe. But I would be disappointed too if you did not reach out for what you wanted in life, in little as well as big things.

"If you have got the impression from me that mistakes are bad, let's try to learn new ways to deal with them together. They're only a waste if you let them make you feel bad about yourself, instead of letting them teach you new ways to get better at whatever it is you tried.

"How about if I tell you a few mistakes I have felt bad about and then you can tell me some of yours if you want to."

If you get something like, "Ah, come on, Dad (Mom)," don't get discouraged.

Just keep it light and share one short story about something silly or stupid you did as a child.

Even if you get no response now, the next time around will be easier for you both.

Learning From Mistakes

If a child is punishing himself for a poor performance with perjoratives like "stupid" or "dumb," you might say, "You're feeling stupid right now because you didn't study enough to get a satisfying grade on your test (or you didn't speak to your friend soon enough about the dance, etc.). That's perfectly natural. It may have been a dumb thing to do. Only you know that.

"But if you figure that out, then you aren't that dumb, are you? Don't forget the difference between being dumb and doing dumb things. I know and I hope you know you were never dumb. And I know you and I both will continue forever to do occasional dumb things."

Bucking Authority

When a child rejects the teaching or authority of a person you would like them to follow and obey, you might say, "You don't like doing what he tells you. Can you identify what it is about the way he teaches or treats you that gives you that feeling? Maybe there is something you or I or he could change to correct the problem. We don't have to know the answer before we explore the question. Let's give it a try."

Drawing Your Boundaries

When you want time for yourself and get confused by the apparent paradox that taking regular, small increments of time for yourself helps you share yourself more with your child, you might say, "I need a little time to myself. I am discovering that I am in a better mood with you and listen to your needs and wants better when I feel good about myself. When I am going in so many directions all the time, I need this time to pull myself together, to focus and integrate myself. Painting my nails (reading the sports section, etc.) gives me a good feeling that will help me respond better to you the rest of the day."

Or for a younger child, "I seem to be getting impatient (angry, bossy, frustrated, crazy) about what's going on between us. I need a few minutes of quiet time to get myself positive and calm again. Can I do something with you for a few minutes to help you get started on something you can do while I am off by myself?"

Up Front About Recovery

When you want specifically to talk about your recovery but want to stay aware that your problems belong to you and should not burden your child, you might say, "I am working hard on myself right now to understand what negative messages I learned as a child and how to replace them with positive messages I know now are true as an adult.

"These are not like information, but more like how to feel and express my feelings in response to life.

"I am trying to bring more contentment into my life. You are very much involved in this process for me, because you mean so much to me and I want to feel close to you. But I don't want to burden you with these problems that I must overcome within me.

"I will be trying to change some of the ways I act with you. And you can help me by telling me if my words or behavior bother you and how you feel about it. If I have been insensitive about your feelings or it has been risky for you to express them, this is one of the things I am trying to change.

"And I ask you in advance to forgive me when you do try to share and I slip back into old negative patterns. It's bound to happen but I hope we can laugh about it, once we've cooled down."

Rejection Again?

When your child rejects your overtures and gives no time or attention to your attempts to share, you may get a flood of feelings, not the least of which may be *déjà vu* of rejection. You might say, "I feel rejected when you respond like that. You feel impatient with me because in the past I have not been as responsive to you as I would have liked, or you would have liked.

"I ask that you be patient with me now because I am trying to change this. I no longer feel I have to be a perfect parent. Instead I know that our relationship is most important to me, and I think we can grow to feel closer without stepping on each others' toes as much as we used to think we would."

The Power Of Words

These conversations may sound unrealistic or impossible to you or they may sound very familiar, depending on the current tone of your parenting relationship. You may think your child is too young, too old, too inexperienced, too independent, too set in her ways.

But in my experience with hundreds of families, these words are effective with children from one year old to 50. The power in these sharings is in their focus on the relationship, that third spiritual entity that we create together. It has a life of its own that either one of us has the power to nurture at will.

Working Behind The Scenes — On Yourself

If you can't imagine yourself saying these things to your child, I recommend you rehearse a little each morning or last thing at night. Try to imagine your child responding not in some ideal way (our ideal, if we have one, is rarely as splendid as the real response which will eventually come), but just as himself. Just as you know him right now, what's the best response he might come up with if you hit on a good moment? Rehearse with that picture in your mind.

Rehearse with children in the checkout line at the supermarket if the parent doesn't look too stand-offish. Rehearse with the mail clerk at the post office or anyone else where you really don't care too much if they think you are weird as a result.

Then let go of the whole idea. Don't allow any tension to build up while you look for the "right opportunity." Instead, expect to have false starts, rebuffs from the child, and rebuffs from yourself. Any words you can bring yourself to say that vaguely relate to your rehearsed thoughts will be progress.

Knowing When To Stop

The hardest thing at first will be to stop after you have delivered your planned words. You will want to fall back on defenses or manipulations so that you won't have to take full responsibility for your feelings and words as you have expressed them. Be patient with yourself when this happens and also notice that nothing as bad as what you dreaded happens as a result of your new approach.

Then wait, attentively, patiently and with faith in the ultimate power of the parent-child bond, for the child's input. It is not essential that we get any. If we continue this kind of communication, we will eventually build an atmosphere of security and acceptance strong enough to push through any dam of defenses that our child may have developed.

Expect to flip-flop, to feel stupid, to want to go back to the old way. But don't get fearful of these feelings either. There is good news and bad news. The bad news is that you can't go back. The good news is the same. Once you have tasted the sweetness of parental self-esteem, the old way will never be as comfortable as it once was. Priest and novelist Andrew Greeley's novel about spiritual awakening, *Patience Of A Saint,* deals masterfully with this issue.

Treat yourself with humor, patience, kindness and faith.

If you are truly working on recovery and building your independence, then you will inevitably be sharing your recovery with your child. The time you spend on your parent-child relationship will be a direct contribution to your recovery just as your recovery is a direct contribution to your child. Practicing a recovering state of mind in your parenting interactions will be more efficient than anything else you do to make you into the parent and the person you want to be.

A Stitch In Time

You may be fearful of the time that these interactions will take and wonder how to get your child to stay still long enough to try them. Or you may think such conversations are entirely too serious for your child to tolerate.

But being given the time and being taken as seriously as any other part of our adult lives is a great compliment to a child. They seldom reject it even if they exhibit no great enthusiasm.

Also dealing with problems before a crisis comes allows you a better chance to deal with it in your new frame of mind rather than when old buttons are being pressed and strings pulled.

The bonus is that if you have these serious chats from time to time, you will save time. Much less time will be spent on poor decisions, indecisions, transgressions, accusations and parries, regrets and frustrations. There will be more time for shared joy, peace, play, fun and mutual appreciation.

Getting Your Spouse On Your Side | 15

Adult children of alcoholics are attracted to people as mates who occurred in the same birth order. They tend to be alike in their world view and many of their co-dependent reactions. This tends to hide the fact that in the new couple and family they create together, they will develop a new dynamic.

An informal survey of couples you know will reveal that youngest children are drawn to each other and first-borns are mutually attracted. Kids from the middle gravitate together too.

Attractions By Sibling Order

The youngest seek to enjoy life, now that they have access to the power that they imagined their parents and older siblings had but that they never had themselves.

Fun-loving and childlike when they meet and court, one or the other may become super-responsible when family duties arrive. Two clowns cannot run a family, one reasons. Someone must get serious.

This shift can shock the other spouse, who increases the gap between them by responding in his or her habitual way, becoming more outrageous, light-hearted, zany and even irresponsible.

Likewise when two oldest children marry, they are attracted most often by their perfectionism and workaholic ambitions. As parents, they have every intention of being easy-going and of giving their children the nurturing atmosphere they felt they missed.

But their ambition coupled with the desire to let kids be kids manifests in some strange results. There is a high level of vicarious ambition. They can be gravely disappointed if their children do not achieve as well as they did because then they do not have the chance, they think, to give the praise and approval they always wanted so much to get and now to give.

Also, these parents often combine education and play in ways that usurp the child's right to play. This hidden agenda has been reinforced in recent years by the school system. It could be said that a whole generation since the 1960s has been raised in this pattern. The deceptive atmosphere creates an aversion to learning, a poor concept of play and even learning disability.

Often too, the mixed messages of the first-born couple force the child to grow up too quickly, the same problem the first-born parents had, though for very different reasons.

The first-born parents adjust to each other just as do the last-born parents. There are too many conflicts with two standard-setting authorities in the house. One usually assumes a subordinate role, rationalizing that her or his standards can't compete with the other's. She or he plays the rescuer instead of the intimidator, which role is left for the other.

One usually sides with the child when the other sets too high standards, pressures the child or gives ambivalent messages that are confusing to the child. The other parent feels betrayed and isolated, feelings already too familiar.

When two middle children marry, they both crave the attention their older siblings always seemed to have. When courting, they both get lots of attention and give it freely because they value it so much. Later, when their children become a major focus of attention, they feel the all too familiar feelings of being second-class and unappreciated.

Most often, one or the other of these born-in-the-middle parents will switch to a different role, as authoritarian or perfectionist like an older sibling or as happy-go-lucky, easy-to-please fun-lover, like a younger sibling.

Scrambled Roles, Co-dependent Pressures

Even if the marriage is not matched according to attractions by birth order, if you or your spouse are from a co-dependent family, there is likely to be some role adjustment and switching around that may not coincide with your natural personalities. These incongruencies will cause tension in the family and tend to repeat co-dependent patterns.

For the children of all these marriages, unless the parents discard their assumed roles and get in touch with themselves through recovery, the key elements of co-dependency will be recreated by these shifting roles and assumed patterns, no matter how much the parents seek to avoid a repeat of the cycle.

Someone who appeared to be just like you at your wedding may ultimately react to you in a way that is opposite to what you expected or would have predicted. Their behavior may resemble parental or sibling patterns that you were sure you had avoided.

What's more, this shift, or the recognition of it, often first appears when you have your own children, when you least want any extra surprises.

Ironically the parents' heartfelt dedication to giving their children a better shake than they had drives them to more fiery conflicts, desperate manipulations and adamant stances. This is a major reason why children have the power to solidify some or destroy other marriages. It most likely has nothing to do with the kind of children they are. It is the way they restimulate their parents' frustrations, fears and insecurities.

Despite all these pitfalls in the relationship between parents, you do not have to wait until your spouse agrees with you on anything at all before you move ahead with recovery.

To be sure, there is no guarantee against fireworks. In fact, it is most likely that your relationship will not stay the same. But it is true that if you continue your recovery, your relationship will change for the better, just as will your relationship with your child.

The most important thing to remember is that you are making changes for you — not for your child, not for your spouse, not for your parents.

The changes are for you because you have no business making choices for anyone else, not even your child or spouse.

Parental Fantasies For The Future

You may want to be proud of your child. You may want to be at his wedding. You may want to hold her hand when she gives birth to your grandchild. But none of these things will be accomplished by your making the child's choices for him or her.

It is so easy to think that if you want to have a wonderful grandchild you must see that your spouse's plans and procedures are the same as yours, that your child achieves, marries well, takes your advice, lives close by, etc., etc.

But first things come first. You have almost no control over these events if you try to work through your child. He or she is likely to resist your control and act unpredictably.

Instead, direct your efforts to your part in the future event.

1. **Take care of yourself.** Keep yourself healthy enough to be there when there is a grandchild.
2. **Trust your child as far as possible** while protecting her from unacceptable risks. Trust the natural human process by which each generation seeks to share its life with the one that came before if relations are comfortable.
3. **Build the link between you.** Work on your relationship so that you will be invited to get to know the grandchild. Practice acceptance, listening, enthusiasm, validation.
4. **Leave others to mind their own business.** Leave your spouse to his own devices. The first three steps are more than enough.

Whether enjoying a grandchild or any other goal occupies your long-range fantasy for the future, these four steps together will be most likely to accomplish it to the maximum extent of your power to influence the event.

The Control Triangle

In any family there are always two parents as far as the child is concerned, even if there has been divorce, separation, adoption or death. The child's relationship with the other parent is essentially beyond your control.

The more time and energy you infuse into trying to control their relationship, the more out of control you will get with respect to your own. The essence of co-dependency is that you mistakenly try to control the uncontrollable.

I like to think of the child and parents as a triangle. Each person is at a point of the triangle. Expectations, communication, caring, enjoyment, humor, put-downs, an infinite variety of interpersonal energy is flowing back and forth constantly between each point and the other two.

You can have significant influence over this flow to both of the other points from yours. The two sides touching your point rely a great deal on your attitudes, behavior, energy and projections.

But you do not have any direct control over the side opposite your point that runs between the child and his other parent. That line does not even touch you.

The sooner you can accept this powerlessness over the other parent's relationship to the child, the better.

This does not mean that you must tolerate what you find intolerable. Your peace of mind and your devotion as parent to your child should exclude any tolerance for child abuse by your spouse, for example, either by words or action. But if you know the limits of your power over their relationship, you will have a better grasp of your multiple options.

You are not obliged to prevent every conflict or even to help resolve it. An Al-Anon saying goes, "Neither create nor avoid a crisis." If the child is not threatened with any serious harm, you may choose simply to withdraw from an unpleasant scene.

Know Your Motives

No matter what you choose to do, it is most important that you know why you are doing it. If your motive is to make your spouse a better parent, to show him what he should be doing, to steer him to better parenting behavior or to show him what he is doing wrong, watch out. The situation will quickly get out of your control and is likely to have unpredictable and unwanted consequences.

Likewise, if your motive is to protect your child from all conflict, from thinking ill of your spouse or from knowing the truth about her, such as the intensity of her feeling, her potential for ruthlessness, uncaring, authoritarianism or whatever — watch out again. You have no control over the effects of your intervention on your child. He may fear that you think he is incapable of handling his relationships, for example, a very negative message.

The most we can do is be there if one or the other of the pair reaches out for some guidance or help in interpretation. Even then we must guard our words or actions carefully, using "I" messages and avoiding judgment, criticism or accusation.

The only motives that will lead us to constructive action or words are those relating to our own serenity and to our two relationships. If you choose your behavior for any of the four reasons above — to take care of yourself, to trust your child as far as possible while protecting her from unacceptable risk, to build a healthy relationship with child or spouse or to let others handle their own affairs — then go ahead.

To illustrate, you might leave a nasty shouting match between your son and his dad in order to take care of yourself. Their behavior disturbs your tranquility of mind, and you choose not to be disturbed. You might explain this to them or not if you feel comfortable doing so.

Or you might stay around in case of some possible escalation but generally ignore the goings on, because, knowing your child's current level of maturity, you trust him to do a better job taking care of himself than you could do for him by intervening.

Or you might intervene if the child has sought your help and you trust him to know when he needs help.

Or you might intervene to protect your child against unacceptable risk. Your link to him as parent, responsible for his physical and emotional safety, is among the healthiest of motives, of course.

Or you might choose not to intervene in order to protect your link with your spouse. In this case, be sure of your true priorities.

If you do not move to help your child because you put peace within the marriage above the immediate protection of a child who needs it, you will find sooner or later that your relationship to your spouse will suffer anyhow because of the blow to your self-esteem when you tolerate intolerable behavior towards your child.

As long as you take time to know why you are inclined to act or not to act, you will know what to do. Avoid all the lectures, accusations, threats, instructions, lessons and warnings that so often add resentment between parents to an already troubling event with a child.

Avoid inviting whatever negativity is in their relationship to poison your relationships with each of them.

It's better to move in quickly when you must and get out quickly, with generous projections of respect for both child and spouse in their freedom of choice within tolerable limits.

The most positive influence we can have on our child's relationship with our spouse is to maintain our direct links in good order and set an example of genuine communication. If we do this, they will tend to come to us more often for guidance and interpretation.

The beauty of the recovery process is that our model will inevitably affect that third side of the triangle which is beyond our control. We cannot put energy into a good link with our child without having a positive effect on the child's self-esteem. This inevitably leads to more positive projections by the child in all directions, including along the link to his other parent.

The same holds true for our spouse and his self-esteem. If we work on building a sound, healthy link to our spouse that promotes his self-esteem as well as ours, his relationships are likely to improve without any intervention from us.

Comparing Parenting Strategies

Showing respect for the independence of your spouse's relationship to your child does not mean that you do not discuss parenting. Far from it. You can use "I" messages to share important feelings — both positive and negative — about your shared parenting experiences. And it can help a great deal to coordinate your parenting styles as thoroughly as possible.

But where there are differences, it's best to agree to disagree, so long as the differences are not contrary to your deepest values as a parent. A running battle between parents over parenting styles is only an invitation to manipulation by the child.

If a behavior is intolerable to you, your efforts at building your self-esteem and your family links will pay off. You will have the courage you will need to seek help and to make the changes necessary to make life tolerable again.

If you want to bring up the issue of how a particular situation was handled, you might say, "I felt very uncomfortable when you were swearing at Freddy this morning. I would appreciate it if you could find a calmer way to express your frustration to him."

Or, "I felt disturbed by the intensity of your anger at Angela this morning. Is there anything I can do to help you lighten your resentment?"

If these comments sound sarcastic or unrealistic, take them one step at a time. Imagine when they could be said if your relationship were such that they could be said in earnest and taken in the right spirit. Then when these situations arise, rehearse later to yourself what you might have been comfortable saying, and try it next time. There is always another chance.

Begin these conversations when tempers are cool and preferably when the child is not there. If there are any adult child issues for your spouse, he or she will tend to play to the audience for different defensive or manipulative effects and communication will be stifled between you.

Candor And Openness

Share openly with your spouse what you are trying to accomplish. This helps prevent unnecessary confusion and misinterpretation. Decide together ahead of time on a quiet time to discuss parenting and personal goals for change in the realms under your control. And limit the amount of time to be spent in the discussion.

For example, you might say, "I have been getting more and more distressed about the way you interact with Jessica. I need to tell you my feelings about it without judging you. I would like to take a half-hour on Saturday morning to talk. If that is not a good time, what would be best for you?"

Don't give up if there is resistance. Simply move to the new level, always with "I" messages. "I am sorry that you are unwilling to discuss parenting issues with me. I need to talk about them because I put a high value on consistency and on acknowledging a child's increasing independence (or whatever). Please tell me how I can make it easier for you to talk about this with me and when you can give me some time."

Remember, your spouse may well have co-dependent elements from childhood. This kind of approach may be entirely new and may create uneasiness and suspicion. Stay with it.

Avoid diagnosing or analyzing your spouse, no matter how obvious the co-dependent patterns appear to you. Just keep yourself and your links to child and spouse clearly at the center of your purpose. Leave their inner lives and their relationship up to them.

Stresses will develop as you change, just like continental plates moving against each other. But gradual adjustments and acceptance of change help avoid earthquakes, and the environment will be more peaceful and enjoyable as a result.

Though we have dealt here primarily with the potential problems of having a spouse who does not share your recovery mode, there are equally impressive satisfactions in developing and implementing positive parenting strategies with your spouse or parenting partner.

Do celebrate even the smallest steps forward and affirm any moves your spouse makes in a salutary direction. A comment like, "I admire the way you handled Bill's request just now," will do much to increase your spouse's cooperation. Do your best to catch your spouse doing well, rather than doing poorly in his parenting. Look for the good and enjoy it. For that is love.

The same moves that build your personal recovery as an adult child raising children will do the most to increase the likelihood of getting the support of your spouse. In each relationship in your life, you will find fertile ground for spreading the love and health that is growing in your life.

Dealing With Others' Reactions To Your Parenting

16

What can you do about others' reactions to your parenting when you are working on your recovery and making changes that people will notice?

Among the hundreds of people around the country I've spoken with about parenting styles and making changes, one of the most frequent concerns is the gratuitous advice, comments and criticisms of others, especially parents, in-laws and teachers and, to a lesser extent, counselors and health professionals.

These well-meaning advisers will not always appreciate the changes you are making, for any of these reasons:

1. They fail to notice anything that needs fixing. They confuse usual and normal with healthy. Since there is nothing dramatically unusual in your family, they advise against change.

   Yet the National Drug Council estimates that there are over 10 million alcoholics in the country and that each one affects at least five other people. Likewise, national figures show that there are more than 30 million adult children of alcoholics. Must we ignore a problem because it is so common?

2. They may be fearful because change always involves the risk of the unknown. They feel safer advising against it so that they will not be blamed if it works out badly.

3. They may be most comfortable with patterns as they are because of their own co-dependent history.

4. They may mistakenly assume that you, as the parent, are responsible for the inner life as well as the outer life of your
child. They believe the myth that children need to be molded
into worthwhile beings and don't come that way. They fear that
your respectful attitude may raise self-indulgent hoodlums.
5. They may fail to realize how worthless and potentially destructive unsolicited advice can be, even given with the best of
intentions, because of the vulnerable self-esteem of adult children raising children.

Responding To Critics

We often try to analyze our critics in order to find out whether
we need to pay attention to them. Are they experts? How much do
they know? How much do they care? Have they given us good
advice before?

But we often forget to ask some much more important questions.
Have they experience in raising healthy, confident, connected children? Do they respect our freedom to make our own decisions? Are
they building or attacking our self-esteem? Are they trying to run
our lives just as they would have us run our children's? Do they
apply their expertise to guide or to control?

There is a multi-leveled aspect to criticism. If the manner in
which advice is offered is not consistent with the manner in which
we are seeking to give advice to our children, then we know right
away that our adviser will not appreciate what we are trying to do.

Instead of trying to figure out where our critics are coming from,
we may need to notice instead their manner of dealing with us.

For example, we may give a more welcoming ear to an in-law
who says, "I feel rejected when Sam never lets me hug him," than
to one who says, "You should tell Sam that good little boys hug
their grandmothers."

Or you may want to respond more eagerly to a teacher who says,
"I am concerned because Mara is slacking off in her work," than if
she were to say, "Your family is just too easy-going about homework."

We have the option of not listening to any unsolicited comments
on our parenting. Many of us have been advice collectors, adding
up the different suggestions from books, relatives, friends and so
forth. We even carry a list in our minds of those who advised
certain behavior, to help us justify it against other critics later.

If we reject all comments categorically, we may help bring ourselves back into balance.

But if we decide to isolate ourselves from unasked-for advice, we must be sure we ask for advice when we need it. We had better be confident that we are sensitive to any problems and that we address them promptly and constructively, including seeking help from capable sources of our choice when indicated.

Asking for help may be one of the most difficult things for you to do as an adult child raising children. Often in the family of origin, asking for help was judged as a sign of weakness. A powerful rationalization for not seeking help for addiction, this myth is usually a closely held conviction with children of co-dependency.

Now as adults, we see that asking for help is an act of wisdom and strength, based on high self-esteem and self-knowledge.

Of course if the person offering advice has a direct relationship with your child, you may want to respond to the situation even if you intend to ignore the advice. For example, you could ignore the unasked-for criticisms of a doctor you see once a year but a teacher who has control over your child for six hours every day may develop a dangerous grudge if she feels ignored.

Re-educating Our Critics

We also have the option of helping our critics to rephrase their comments in a manner that is more respectful of our freedom of choice. Sometimes this has the salutary effect of making the criticism dissolve before the very eyes of the critic.

For example, if your in-law said, "Why don't you ever listen to me?" you might respond, "You seem concerned that I don't listen to you." The silence that usually follows this exchange is awesome. By our response we have demonstrated that we are listening very well, thank you.

At the least our gracious request to have the criticism recast in more acceptable form lets the critic know for the future what form will please us more.

Don't be afraid to restate what critics have said in a more acceptable way. They may or may not see the difference, but they will feel it, beneficially. With a little practice this is one of the most effective ways to handle unwanted comments.

When your mother says, "Jim should wash his hands more often," you might respond, "You would be more comfortable if Jim came to your table with his hands washed."

Or if a teacher says, "Sarah has a poor attention span," you might say, "You are concerned because Sarah has not been paying enough attention to you in class."

This kind of careful listening and reflecting back on the feeling level defuses the negative energy of the critical message. It switches the mood from accusation and defense to sharing of a problem and cooperative seeking of solutions.

How To Benefit From Criticism

An added benefit of rephrasing criticism is that it often helps us discover how to meet the criticism. In the grandmother example, we might at first feel guilt and burden, thinking that we have to take on one more chore of reminding Jim to wash more often. When we rephrase the criticism, we discover that all we have to do is remind him to wash before dinner when we are at grandma's.

Likewise in the teacher's case, we may run fears through our mind that Sarah has a problem, may develop a learning disability and may need a series of tests or counseling. When we rephrase the criticism, we keep it at the precise level of its current significance. All we need to do now and perhaps ever, is suggest to Sarah that she pay more attention to that particular teacher.

A great temptation in these exchanges with advisers is to follow up your reflective response with some well-worn defenses, explanation or accusations, just to cover all the bases. But instead, try to let the reflection do its work without any follow-up. Sharing our immediate feelings and hearing and reflecting back theirs is the quickest way to build communication.

Criticisms couched in negative terms always come from the negative feelings of the speaker, not from anything we have said or done. Remember that you have no power to change their negative attitudes. But you do have the power to change your own responses to them and to influence the tone of the relationship. As one bit of Al-Anon literature states, no one says you have to take offense just because it is offered.

Most important of all with gratuitous criticism is to keep it from preoccupying you. So often adult children raising children are people-pleasers. This is one reason we collect advice. We want to balance all the suggestions and do enough of each so that no one can accuse us of being stupid, thoughtless, irresponsible or selfish.

Often even when we reject advice out of hand, we let it haunt us later. In the grandparent example, each time we would think of having Jimmy wash his hands, we would feel less capable as parents because we would recall the mental tape of parental criticism.

We need to detach from our old mind-games and deal with the issue at the precise level that is appropriate. Then if there is some merit to the criticism, we can integrate it into our decision-making processes without accepting it as a wound to our recovering self-esteem as parents.

If we would ideally have Jimmy wash more often, we can re-assess our present priorities and see if it is important enough to us to mention it to him or take other steps to increase its likelihood. Perhaps he would like to shop for a fancy bar of soap, for example.

If we are not interested ourselves in more washing, we can let it go entirely.

Whatever our decision, we need not go back and communicate it to the critic. If someone offers unasked-for advice, they are throwing it to the wind and can expect no return on their investment. We are also free to be appreciative and grateful for the good intention and still ignore or apply the advice as freely as we wish, without obligation to report our action or results.

If you want to report back, you can. But know your motives. If it is an old habit of "absolute honesty" with a parent, watch out. It is instead an invitation to manipulation. If it is to stave off later comments, to let the other know you've taken care of it, watch out again. Our fears and our desire to control the critic's future behavior is motivating us and like a self-fulfilling prophecy, we might well increase the meddling rather than reduce it.

Co-dependent Relatives

Often your relatives are still in the alcoholic or co-dependent family pattern and will find endless fault with your changing approach. Or you may interpret their silence as continuous criticism because they never say anything nice. Or you might even be desperately hopeful that they will notice the change, like it and even learn by it.

Relatives may have no comprehension of what you are doing, and many recovering adult children raising children talk themselves blue in the face trying to help relatives understand.

They may not comprehend it because they think parenting without control and manipulation is boring (no lively repartee etc.) or no parenting at all (no authority and obedience).

Or they may see a ready excuse to complain about you in order to reinforce old resentments and keep buried the suppressed love that waits deep within to come out. Which it is should not concern you. You cannot know and it can shift back and forth like lightning.

Our job is to do our best not to analyze or change the critics but to work toward a healthy tone for the relationship we have with them, no matter how tenuous it may be.

As we saw in connection with birth order, in families touched by addiction the breaches between siblings are pandemic. This means that as adult children raising children, our children have little input or contact with uncles, aunts and cousins.

We often hear that time heals. But co-dependent families have a defense against even that. Time is actually merely a series of events. We can make it go very slowly by doing nothing, avoiding events. Or we can speed it up by doing many things, filling our lives with events.

In the family feuds of co-dependent families, a source of complaints can be nurtured indefinitely by avoiding interactive events. By shutting each other off, they avoid the healing process of successive interactive events that would help all to acknowledge the increasing distance from the old destructive interactions and to accept the suppressed love and spiritual bond that links one relative to another.

Of course the feuds are rarely nurtured deliberately. In the co-dependent family, it is usual to project blame and guilt onto a sibling without realizing you are doing so. Some siblings keep each other at a distance all their lives to avoid confronting the guiltlessness of the other or being reminded of the lingering personal pain.

But to allow healing to take place among our extended family, we need to work on developing the courage to take the risk of interaction. If we are not ready to interact without adding another unpleasant incident to the long list adult children often harbor, then we surely must wait. If we want to make a contact with a long-lost relative purely in order to help them, it is best to let it go.

But if we are in touch with our true motivations, we will be able to step back when we meet heavy resistance. We will be able to maintain our equanimity even if we are rebuffed and to feel good about trying again later.

To have a total family healing may take time, sometimes, tragically too long for one lifetime to accommodate. But if you read or listen to histories of families, you discover that they do happen and it takes only one to begin the healing process. That one can be you.

Martha

Martha's eight-year-old son Michael attended a school that gave descriptive reports instead of grades in the early years. His report was suddenly out of sync with earlier ones. The report stated that the child was feeling isolated from his friends and hopefully would overcome his loneliness.

Martha, an adult child in recovery, discussed the issue with her husband who was supportive of her recovery efforts and parenting style. She felt in good communication with her son and believed she would have heard of such a problem if it existed.

They set an appointment with the teacher Rachel to discuss it. Rachel said that she had changed her impression of Michael after a school psychologist had had an interview with each of the children as part of a special new service offered by the school.

The psychologist had reported that a tiff on the playground one day had caused a breach among the boys. The boys had been teasing a girl and Michael had separated himself from them, not being comfortable with the intensity of the sexist teasing. The boys did not include him in their play for the rest of the day. The psychologist's interview happened to be that afternoon. In the course of the talk she asked him if he felt lonely and isolated. He answered, "Well, yes."

When Martha heard the story, she remembered Michael telling her about it that day. He had related how a couple of the boys got really stupid and were nasty to the girl, with whom he got along fine. He also had mentioned that he played by himself the rest of the day.

The mother explained to the teacher that Michael had been raised in a way that encouraged him to be in touch with his feelings moment to moment, to be unafraid to express them and to make his choices based on what he was comfortable with. She explained that the child's responses with his friends and with the psychologist were in both cases good signs in this context.

Rachel agreed that this view was more in line with her own impression of the boy's social health and had another talk with the psychologist. The report was rewritten.

Martha later reviewed the entire matter with Michael, who laughed at the strange doings of well-meaning adults and hurried back to his playing.

When To Intervene

When we have reached some level of dialogue with our children about our family attitudes in recovery, we may find it necessary to do the same with outside authorities, especially if they have expressed either joy or concern over our children's behaviors. This is to help protect the children from negative consequences of our efforts when these consequences are likely to be incomprehensible to them.

You must assume that outsiders may see new stresses in your children as you go through changes. A quiet child may get suddenly disruptive, a rebellious child may become sullen and withdrawn.

Our changes are unsettling to our children. No sooner have they developed sophisticated defense mechanisms, we change the rules on them. It takes time for them to discover that rules are no longer the thing that has strongest sway over family relations. Or we begin talking about "feelings" and they don't even have what we can call a "feeling" vocabulary.

This is one reason why it is important to share our recovery process with our child: To be absolutely clear about what we are trying to do for ourselves and for our relationship with them and to be persuasive that no matter how it may look at times, they are not the cause or source of any of the trouble, and if they feel that they may be, we would like them to say so.

Keep in mind that while a kindergartner may not be able to appreciate the long-term risks of a teacher's grudges or negative judgment and may need our intervention, a teenager does not need as much protection.

We would do better to explore with our teenager the consequences of an evolving student-teacher relationship than to try to interject ourselves directly between them.

Like the triangle in the last chapter, we cannot change the child-teacher relationship directly but only by building the self-esteem of each individually in our relationship with them, by setting an example of better communication and by being available to help with interpretation if asked, as in Martha's case.

When you change, it is ultimately inevitable that your child will change too. If growing pains become noticeable to others, take it as a sign that you need to stay attentive or be more attentive to your child. If the authority is receptive, share with them that the situation is a temporary adjustment and that you would like to check back with them later at some predetermined time.

If they are not receptive, that is all right too. If the stresses are more than your child can handle, investigate options — from changing sections in schools, to a vacation, to changing schools, neighborhoods, doctors or other.

More often than not, a child can handle new stresses at school quite well if she is allowed to express feelings openly and genuinely at home and knows that we will respect her relationships with others while coming to her aid if she asks.

Modeling Responses To Criticism

Be candid with your child about how and why you are no longer swayed unduly by criticism. Have no fear that if the child sees you disregard your parent's advice, he will be more likely to disregard yours. Trust the bond you are nurturing. Your candor achieves these valuable effects:

1. You will bolster your own self-esteem by sharing your positive progress with someone you love.
2. You will be modeling for your child a more constructive way to deal with the opinions of others, one of the most important skills we can have as adults in this society.
3. You will be increasing his sense of security by demonstrating that you are in control of your life and are making your parenting choices not in a vacuum or an overwhelming cacophony of opinions, but in an atmosphere of serenity and confidence.
4. You will be supporting his self-esteem by affirming that he has no guilt in the matter, that he need not please both you and your critics and that you want to share your thoughts with him.

Crowding Out The Critics

A last important tool for dealing with others' reactions to your parenting is to surround yourself with people who do support your efforts to change for the better.

If spouse, family, teachers or counselor do not understand, there are others out there who will. It is amazing how meaningful just an hour a week can be with someone or a group who can share your hopes and ambitions for growth.

Unlike our relatives, we can pick and choose our friends and associates. Seek out counselors and others who make you feel good about your power to change for the better, who inspire you to add another goal to your vision of recovery, and who welcome other sources of reinforcement in your life besides their own.

In recent years self-help groups have grown tremendously and are easier than ever to find. Just be sure to get the real thing. Some spin-off groups have a short brilliant life, thinking they can make progress with short-cuts and without accepting certain truths, like your powerlessness over another person's life, the necessity of letting go of problems to get solutions and the need for some explicit component that addresses our wounded spirits.

If you are in a group that seems bogged down on one of these topics, invest your healing energy for a time if you like. But if the drain is too great, move on. You will be wonderfully surprised by the support and encouragement you will get from people who can share with you not only common experiences but also the hope and strength they have built through their recovery.

Each of us has a unique path to spiritual independence. Sharing the path for a time with a child has to be one of the greatest privileges on earth.

Affirmations For Adult Children Raising Children

17

Affirmative messages that we tell ourselves can be a powerful tool in the recovery program from the co-dependent syndrome of the adult child raising children.

Affirmations will help you substitute new self-empowering thoughts for the old tired thoughts you are now letting go. Filling your head with positive messages about you, your children, your relationships, your parents and your past is extremely effective in crowding out the negative messages you may have saved from long ago.

You can use affirmations in many different ways. Read them all through, or just pick a couple that seem particularly apropos right now. Or underline your favorites and work on them until others begin to appeal to you.

Say them to yourself or read them aloud. Repeat them on a walk or while driving. Say them to a close friend or fellow in recovery. Write one that seems unbelievable to you, over and over again, until disbelief and negativity disappear.

Share some affirmations with your children or spouse. Or have someone read them to you, substituting "you" or your name for "I."

Any and all of these uses will help. Choose whichever is comfortable for you today. Then keep it up daily and when you feel ready for more or for a change, come back to this chapter and choose other affirmations or methods of using them.

For General Self-Esteem

I deserve to spend time with myself, a little each day.

I am getting better and better.

I will set reasonable goals for myself.

I will set goals that are consistent with my higher values in life.

I can become what I most deeply admire.

I am an integrated whole of body, mind and spirit.

My words and behavior are coming every day more in line with my highest values.

I set aside time each day to become ever more conscious of my values.

I am grateful for my life, my feelings, my power and my connectedness to the universal reality.

I hold myself in high esteem because I am a part of the universal reality and force for good.

I strive for excellence, not perfection, on my highest priorities of life.

I delegate to others whenever possible those things that are not important enough to motivate me to excellence.

I forgive myself freely for the ignorance and negativity that led to past mistakes and injuries to myself or others.

I forgive all those who have not met my wants the way I wanted them to.

I am manifesting each day my increasing awareness of my spiritual connectedness with life.

For Acknowledgment And Acceptance

I acknowledge that I am part of a larger whole and share in the life force that creates all events in the universe.

I am in the right place at the right time doing the right thing according to the grand plan of the universe which is a matter of faith, not knowledge.

I accept that my life has included both pain and pleasure and that I am entitled to feel and harmlessly express all associated emotions.

I acknowledge the efforts of family, teachers and all those who have loved, cared for and taught me over the years.

I accept that the efforts of family, teachers and others were not always perfect, successful or adequate to my needs.

I accept that each person in my life was and is responsible for his or her words and actions no matter what provocation or excuse may have appeared to justify them.

I accept responsibility for my past life choices, words and actions, and acknowledge in each case that I did the best I could with the knowledge, skills and maturity available to me at the time.

I accept that my words and actions have not always been and are not now always perfect, successful, ideal or constructive.

I accept that my desire for unconditional love, my expectation of mutual support from people, and my caring feelings for others are natural, normal, healthy and ultimately welcomed by others at the spiritual level.

I acknowledge my growth so far and accept that change will continue at an ever increasing rate.

I accept that I cannot see to the end of the unfolding process of life or even around the next corner.

I accept that I am in control of my life only, and no one else's.

I forgive my parents, relatives, doctors, teachers, employers and others for any negative effects of their words and actions on me and any resulting pain.

I forgive myself for blaming myself for not being able to control their feelings, actions and responses to me.

I forgive myself for the negative effects of my words and actions on me and on others and any resulting pain.

I forgive myself for assuming any blame, guilt, shame or self-limitation out of ignorance or misinterpretation of events around me.

I let go of negative feelings and attitudes about myself and others that interfere with the free flow of positive energy and love between us.

I forgive myself for trying to control the uncontrollable and for tolerating the intolerable.

For My Relationships

I feel close to my true self and appreciate my basic value.

I feel close to those around me.

I do not control others' responses to me.

I am free to change my modes of behavior in light of my increasing experience and knowledge.

My self-esteem is independent of anyone's particular response to me.

I recognize rejection as rejection of my words or actions and not of my self.

I feel comfortable sharing with another my feelings about our relationship.

I am free to say or not say anything I like, knowing that no harm will come if I stay consistent with my highest priorities and with reality, as I perceive it.

I take time to think for myself before I move to words or action.

I listen attentively to others and reflect back the feelings they share.

I gratefully refrain from reading minds, interpreting symbolic behavior, second-guessing or figuring out others.

I respond to stress in a relationship by seeking causes within myself and addressing feelings.

My greatest power with others comes from my empathetic listening and validating communication.

I express my love by looking for the good which is in all people and setting my mind to enjoy it.

I am overflowing with love, which I express in little and large ways each day, toward myself and others.

I refrain from judging, condemning, controlling, criticizing and blaming others.

I encourage and trust others to know their needs and seek my help when they want it.

I am free to let go of or create relationships as I feel comfortable, in light of my highest priorities and deepest intuitions.

I build relationships that are healthy for me, that increase my self-esteem and sense of wholeness and integration.

My reward for loving others is the joy I get from holding them in high spiritual esteem, which affirms our mutual connectedness and my ultimate value in the universe.

I look to myself as a source of healing power in a relationship.

I let go of any intent to change another or push them beyond their comfort zone of acceptable risk.

I forgive myself for unconsciously or consciously imposing my will on others.

For My Relationship With My Child

I see in my children a reflection of the good in the universe.

I see in my children a reflection of the good that is in me.

I forgive myself for any wrong messages, models or attitudes I have expressed to my children.

I forgive my children for any negative messages or behaviors they may have adopted from me or others.

I forgive myself for unconsciously or consciously imposing on my children any stresses, pain or negative messages left over from my own past.

I forgive my parents, relatives, doctors, teachers and all others who may have given my children negative messages, poor models or injury in the past.

I focus today on the things I most like about my child, no matter how inconsequential these things may seem today.

I praise my child freely for the good feelings I get from his or her very existence and presence in my life.

I feel and express empathy for the ups and downs of life as a child.

No matter what my past behavior has been, I am here now for my child.

I am free to reject unacceptable behavior without rejecting my child.

I regularly express my personal and parental wants and needs in a clear, age-appropriate and nonthreatening way to my child.

I accept my child as a spiritual equal, with his (her) own unique purpose and destiny in life.

I willingly let go of any defenses before my child.

My child is exquisitely receptive to my genuine communication.

I communicate respectfully, candidly, genuinely and enthusiastically with my child.

I give and maintain eye contact freely with my child.

I initiate conversation more and more often with an "I" message, stating my present genuine feeling, together with a nonjudgmental statement of the immediate events that relate to my feeling.

I apologize freely and promptly for any words, actions or decisions I regret.

I express candidly to my children, with due regard to age, the reasons beyond their control for any words and actions of mine that may give them concern of any kind.

I do not burden my children with matters beyond their age-appropriate level, nor do I overprotect.

I gratefully liberate my child from any responsibility for my emotional happiness or for the fulfillment of any unmet needs.

I let go of any specific ambitions for my child.

My sole ambition for my child is that she (he) manifest to the fullest her (his) spiritual essence as a loving, joyful, capable human being.

I do not pass judgment on my child or his (her) inner life.

I gratefully let go of any supposed responsibility or duty to figure out the inner life of my child.

I encourage and trust my children to learn their own needs, to express them freely, and to ask for my help whenever they want it.

I wait until asked to give my help except in the case of actual emergency.

I base my parental authority upon a relationship of mutual trust, mentorship and sponsorship with my child.

I accept the parent-child bond as a natural and immutable force for good in my life. I revel in my spiritual connectedness to my child.

I earn the trust and candor of my child by respecting our spiritual equality and sharing myself with him (her).

I accept parental responsibility for protecting my child from only those risks that are either too great, too likely or too incomprehensible for me to be comfortable with, taking into account my child's age, skills, information and maturity.

I recognize the rights of my child to play, to experiment, to make mistakes and to surpass my expectations.

I delegate to my child all decisions that affect her (his) life for which she (he) has the requisite age, information, skill and maturity.

I share with my child all decisions respecting our relationship, taking age-appropriateness into account.

I feel free to make preemptive decisions where the risk of physical, mental or emotional harm to my child is too great or too likely for me to feel comfortable letting the child decide.

I think through my decisions and motives candidly and calmly.

I express to my child in a clear manner my genuine, primary and essential reason for any decision affecting her (him), even when it does not meet my ideal standards for rationality.

I avoid rationalizations, excuses and make-weights, preferring no explanation at all to dissembling.

I feel free to take care of myself physically, mentally, emotionally and spiritually, which helps me become the parent I want to be.

Each day I become more like the parent I want to be.

I forgive myself and my child for using defenses and manipulations to block the free flow of positive energy between us.

I am my child's parent no matter what I do and our bond is there forever.

I am no longer afraid of changing my style of parenting for the better in line with my highest priorities.

I feel free to postpone anything — ambitions, lessons, initiatives or judgments — in favor of staying in line with my personal and parenting values.

My parental love is my greatest gift to my child and I give it freely in my words and deeds.

I accept criticism at the level of its usefulness to me in my ongoing process of self-examination and improvement as a parent.

I reject any attacks, innuendos or criticisms that belittle my value as a person or parent.

My child is infinitely loving, attentive, responsive and caring toward me whether I can detect it or not.

I look for, find, feel, love and enjoy the goodness in my child.

My child is a radiant spiritual being.

My child has more than enough beauty, intelligence, health and spiritual connectedness to accomplish all that he (she) desires, and to make me proud.

I am the proud parent of my child just exactly as he (she) is today.

I welcome the positive energy of the universe to assist me in becoming the parent that I want to be and that will best meet the needs of my child.

I am safe from despair because parental love fills my heart.

My child and I are safe and secure at all times.

I show my parental affection freely and appropriately. I listen attentively to my child, who is the best and only judge of his needs.

My child finds ways to express his (her) needs to me if I make myself available in mutual trust.

I do not need to substitute for any other person in my child's life, whether divorced spouse, teacher, doctor, sibling or other, nor do I feel displaced by these.

My child's greatest need of me is to have me share my unfolding self with him (her) here and now, as I am becoming today.

My parenting relationship is subject to positive change any time, by energetic input by me or my child.

I always have another opportunity to say or do more of what I wished I had said or done with my child.

I respect my child's right to develop his (her) relationships with others.

I aim not to control my child's relationships, occupations or activities but to gain her (his) trust so that I can express what I am comfortable with, my perception of the risks, my superior experience and my feelings, rational or irrational.

I liberate my child to listen and respond as she (he) sees fit and respect her (his) need for privacy, freedom, responsibility, self-expression and self-determination.

I strive for excellence, not perfection, in my parenting and delegate whenever I can those activities that do not advance me towards that goal.

I respect the increasing maturity of my child and gratefully accept its inevitability.

I am in the perpetual process, which began with birth, of letting go of my child.

I trust my child to know what he (she) must learn at any given time.

I concentrate on being available to assist in finding resources, interpreting and problem-solving, but not controlling in the learning processes and education of my child.

I gratefully acknowledge my child's, as well as my own, right to play — to experiment freely in a low-risk nonjudgmental, self-directed environment, with any ideas, things or events of personal choosing.

I accept my child's, as well as my own, right to take risks, to make mistakes, to compete and to reap meaningful rewards.

I see all those close to me lending their support consciously or unconsciously to my efforts to improve myself and my parenting.

I accept it as my duty not to isolate my child from less than perfect influences but instead to help her (him) interpret them in perspective so as to minimize their harm and maximize their benefit.

I consciously increase my child's vocabulary for feelings, empathy and validation by sharing my positive thoughts, feelings, affirmations and meaningful results with him (her) whenever appropriate.

I let go of any fear that resemblances between my child and me, my parents or others will lead to any harm.

I will celebrate resemblances of my child to myself, my parents or others, as an opportunity to manifest more fully our common spiritual essence.

I accept my freedom to rewrite old parenting tapes, to wipe clean old cloudy blackboards, to build new ways of parenting directly on the spiritual bedrock of the God-given parent-child bond.

I seek out people who share my experiences, strengths and

hopes for a better parenting experience.

I celebrate the likelihood that family matters will work out more exquisitely than I can plan or even imagine.

I act promptly without procrastination, preoccupation, false humility or impostor feelings, on my resolve to grow as parent and person.

I freely share my experience, strengths and hopes with others who will listen as I meet the special challenges of parenting as an adult child raising children.

Parent And Child
Independent
Together

18

Think how many times you have heard or said, "They grow up too fast."

If we learn to live fully in every moment of our parenting, our children don't grow up too fast at all. They grow up at just the right speed.

If we are not completely there, if we are preoccupied by our own unfinished business of childhood, we feel cheated, hurried, pressured. We feel we've missed our turn again!

I like to think of the camera. It's fun to have snapshots of past family occasions, to freeze the action for later appreciation, to make recall of fun moments easy. But how many of us have carried cameras so much that we start to see the events in our lives in terms of whether they would make a good picture? Or as soon as we see a darling pose or a beautiful scene, we run away from it to try to capture it on camera for the future instead of enjoying it now?

Do we really think that looking through our picture album later will give us the same enjoyment that we passed up when we took the quick snapshot and then went back to urgent trivia like cooking, cleaning, answering the telephone or answering a criticism?

As adult children raising children in recovery, we can stop collecting special moments in our lives for future enjoyment when we have got our lives in order. Our children surely grow up too fast for that.

Instead we must enjoy them now. Throw out the camera if need be. Watch them hard and long enough so that you have squeezed every bit of enjoyment out of the moment and emblazoned the image on your mind. If you do that, you will find you have all the time you need to love them.

Patience And Acting "As If"

As we move towards independence through our recovery, we find it easier and easier to forgive others whom we've blamed for our pain, and to forgive ourselves whom we've blamed for being less than perfect. As we find ourselves becoming more and more who we want to be, we hold onto our grudges and self-pity less and less.

Gradually these are replaced with gratitude for the lessons of life, for what we have become and for our parents' sharing of themselves. For, however lame or incomplete or short of perfect their parenting was, we know they did the best they knew how at the time, just as we do now. We can also feel grateful that we do not carry their awful burden of addiction and co-dependency.

With patience and acting "as if," our recovery can proceed quietly within our heads or as demonstratively as we choose, within our comfort zone of acceptable risk. With attention to these strategies, we can begin to share the benefits of our recovery process right away with our children, without burdening them with the details of our transformation.

With patience and acting "as if," we begin to really feel that we have all the time we need to become what we need to be. We discover that our turn has come. We discover that we are at last as independent as we want to be, and we feel as independent as we want to feel at any given moment. To paraphrase Abraham Lincoln, we are just about as happy as we set our minds to be.

We begin to ask for our turn instead of waiting for it and fearing it will not come.

We begin to help others give it to us instead of explaining why it did not come or manipulating someone else into giving up theirs for us.

We discover that if our eyes are wide open we have many more turns in the game of life than we ever dreamed we might be entitled to.

We discover that we need a Higher Power to help us justify our joy instead of to plead with to end our sorrow.

It is indeed our turn to love and be loved, to be ourselves, and to know ourselves by loving another whose very life has been given into our care.

We have seen that we do not have to start from scratch to revitalize our parenting. The natural parent-child bond, uniquely developed in human beings, can be revitalized in one generation, even in a matter of years or months, no matter what our age or the age of our child.

Putting Your Life In Order

You can assess your progress away from co-dependency and toward independence of spirit in your family life by assessing the congruence between your highest spiritual aspirations and the many levels of your daily interactions with your child.

You and your child can look forward to achieving, one day at a time, the goal of two independent people, sharing your lives, helping each other, and exploring your mutual world together, through a bond of love and trust.

When there is a high congruence, your independence is reaffirmed with every interaction. You can't lose for winning.

The multiple levels of interaction occur as follows, beginning with the spiritual:

1. Essential spiritual value and connectedness to the universal good.
2. Attitudes and assumptions emanating from this or another world view.
3. Perceptions from the senses, conscious and unconscious, about the people, places and things around us.
4. Feelings generated in response to interpretations of perceptions based on these attitudes and assumptions.
5. Thoughts and convictions which explain, rationalize or justify our feelings to ourselves or others.
6. Words and behaviors that express — more or less consciously — these feelings, thoughts and convictions.
7. Habits that fill the least aware moments of our lives and that most clearly reveal the basic congruity or misalignment of our world view with the basic reality of our spiritual value.

In our parenting we can check for any misalignments, working backwards from habits that are getting in the way of our parenting through words and actions, rationalizations, feelings, perceptions and attitudes to our basic world view of connectedness and value or isolation and low self-esteem.

With our children, with patience and acting "as if", we can rewrite our future. And it is almost miraculous how they will help us.

A Happy Holiday

To illustrate, when my children were about nine and seven years old, we were having some trouble with our holiday celebration. We had so many traditions and activities everyone wanted to do that we never got to them all. The anticipated frustration and failure to meet our goals was damaging our self-esteem as a family and it started to overshadow the anticipated joys of the season.

The problem threatened to get worse as our children became older and had more definite ideas of what they wanted to do to celebrate the holiday.

To get a perspective on the problem, we parents examined the habits and traditions we had established for ourselves and identified our own personal feelings.

We discovered that many of them had been designed to overcome feelings from our families of origin. Many had outlived their usefulness, our having met those old needs through our recovery.

It was time for some clarity and healing.

We discovered that our present frustration stemmed not from too much to do but from too many old ghosts being maintained symbolically by our habitual behavior.

We began to expose the old feelings and go through a mourning process or a forgiving process wherever we could. Where the old feelings would not yet let go, we helped each other think of simpler, easier ways to satisfy the old needs.

We found that each of us was doing things because we thought others too wanted them even though they hadn't asked. We now asked each other what we most wanted out of the season. We tried to avoid resentments about misplaced efforts and about half-hearted thank you's for unasked for favors.

When these were exposed, we used laughter to release the tension. With all of us sharing our errors, it was not hard to learn the healing power of humor.

I had always baked a great selection of cookies because I had loved doing it with my grandmother. But my children didn't care about the wide variety. They just wanted their two favorites. We found it was much more fun just to make these, without the pressure from other recipes waiting.

To paraphrase Rokelle Lerner's words in *Daily Affirmations,* we risk burnout if we try to give to everyone else what *we* want.

We each made lists of holiday events that meant the most to us, prioritized them and then went around the table like a card game, offering our next priority, while one of us inserted the items in the calendar. This way each person got their first three choices. Then we continued.

We checked the schedule and when it was full enough, other choices were abandoned. For the children, we reviewed the list again to see that a must-do didn't slip away by mistake. Also we left a little leeway for new ideas or resurrected old ones as the special time drew nearer.

This multi-level family process could not have been accomplished without frequent affirmation of the basic goodness, generosity, healing powers and good intent of each, nor without a basic trust that each knew best what he or she wanted and would tell others if the atmosphere were right.

Through this process we found that even the most ingrained symbolism, habits and expectations could be modified in an atmosphere of unconditional love, respect and communication. Our children met us more than halfway and loved finding ways to get to the heart of the seasonal joy and peace.

Myths That Link Us To Reality

Andrew Greeley, Catholic priest, novelist and sociologist, claims that the maturing process has three stages: learning the myths of our elders, rebelling against them, then discovering our own. By myths he means those attitudes and beliefs that shape the way we see the world.

For the adult child raising children, the parental myths were largely nonfunctional, the rebellion was so complete that we defined ourselves by its terms alone, and the discovery of our own mythology is a challenge that touches us to the core.

Before recovery we had been working with a dysfunctional mythology adopted in ignorance by a child in a distorted and unnatural environment. Now in recovery we are creating new myths to connect us to spiritual truth.

No doubt our children will have to rebel and discover their own mythology. But we can hope that the one we are now giving them will require a minimum of rewriting.

Let go of self-imposed duties to make your child turn out right.
Let go of blame you've placed on others for why you did not turn
out right. Accept that you have the power right now to turn out right,
to be content with yourself. Work a little each day to exert that
power in the relationship you are creating with your child.

Today it is your turn.

Sources Of Healing

Our healing is our responsibility, independent of our children.
We are learning in the works of Bernie Siegel, Norman Cousins and
others that successful physical recovery requires almost universally
that the patient take responsibility for his progress and conduct his
own treatment with the help of advisers. So too in the realm of our
spirit, our attitudes and our behaviors, we must take responsibility
to unburden ourselves.

We cannot wait for a sign to appear that a broken leg is mended
before we try to walk again. The only sign is in the increasing grace
and comfort with which we walk.

Likewise we cannot wait for a sign to appear that our spirits are
healed before we try to relate to our child with our new-found
attitudes. The only sign is in the increasing grace and comfort with
which we live our lives and parent our children.

Now You Know . . .

I hope this book has helped you explore the special challenges
you face as an adult child raising your own children. You know how
to recognize your adult child issues in the context of your parenting
and to accept that these will affect your child.

You know the source of the spiritual gap that characterizes adult
children now raising their own, and you know how to close it by
coming to terms with your childhood innocence and powerlessness
and with your parents' chemically induced incapacity to love you as
you deserved.

You know how to let go of generalized self-doubts in order to be
specific about key sensitivity areas in your parenting, including
affection, performance, authority and trust.

You know how to review your own childhood experience constructively and to use in that review your new understanding of what
stage of co-dependent behavior in your family of origin had greatest
impact on your patterns of reactions.

You have learned the effects of not only your parents but also sibling dynamics and birth order on your attitudes and behavior.

You know how to liberate yourself from obsolete messages and tapes by acknowledging your feelings, discovering underlying assumptions, correcting those in light of your careful review and your superior knowledge, forgiving others and yourself and allowing love and gratitude to motivate your new life.

You have developed specific strategies for responding to your children with love, touch and validation rather than with fear of rejection. You can let go of doubts about your lovability and respectability so that you can show your parental love candidly and consistently.

You have new courage and ways to express, assert and take care of yourself that make defenses against others unnecessary. You can find satisfaction in those aspects of your life over which you have control — namely yourself and the tone of your relationship with your child — so that you do not seek to impose inappropriate standards on your child's performance.

You have seen how to replace manipulative techniques with genuine connectedness and communication, to deactivate your buttons and stop pressing others, especially in the area of parental teaching and authority.

You have acquired new tools for dealing with depression and despair by building on your intuitive core of trust in the ultimate goodness of the universe and in your innate spiritual value. You can extend that trust to your child and his or her growing independence, assisted by the indestructible parent-child bond.

You have seen how your recovery — recovery of your self-esteem, your spiritual bond to your parents and others and your rights and power as an individual — benefits your child no matter at what stage you are. You know how to maximize the benefits.

You have been given strategies to achieve maximum satisfaction in your evolving relationships with your children, whether or not your spouse is on the same track, strategies that will at the same time increase the likelihood of his or her cooperation.

You have learned to detach yourself from the hurt of others' criticisms and use your own best judgment of what is right for you and your family, calling for help when you need it.

You have a list of powerful affirmations to keep your energy and enthusiasm high for yourself and your child and to create a vision of meaningful interaction that will tend to be self-fulfilling.

You know how to reconnect with universal reality and your child's spiritual nature by unblocking your learning processes and using the positive reinforcement of your parenting experience. You have learned how to manifest your parental love in ever more meaningful ways with the ever-ready help of your children.

You are launched on what I believe to be one of the most exciting and rewarding adventures of life, participating actively and consciously in the ongoing process of creating the human spirit, one person at a time, one right after another, one helping the next.

What this book can't do for you is substitute for the interactions with your children and others that will help you experience and appreciate your recovery. Healing goes on in the mind. But self-esteem makes leaps and bounds when we share our healthy selves with others.

I urge you to take the risk of loving now.

The great philosopher Goethe said that the infinite variety of Nature came from the metaphysical fact that every creature strives to be the best of its kind. Each tree perceives itself to be *tree*. Each bird strives to be *bird*. Each has a unique interpretation of what it is to be a tree or a bird. And all of life is united in this drive to become what you are at the highest level.

So each child is born with his or her own version of what it is to be a human being. Each one discovers gradually, by living, what his unique interpretation is of this masterful creation. As adult children, we must trust our own unique interpretation and let it out of the old file drawer where it was buried long ago under piles of others' and our own misinterpretations of what we should be.

We must begin to manifest that unique *human being* that we wish to be in each thought, behavior, lifestyle and relationship, to become who we are at the highest level.

And we must free our children, by our love, to do the same.

When you use the tools in this book to heal past hurts, to mend faulty visions of what it is to be parent, child or family and to discover the spiritual core of family connectedness across three generations, your potential to meet your child's needs as a parent and to be the parent you most want to be is altogether magnificent.

Please accept my love, faith, gratitude and enthusiasm for our common quest. And have an excellent adventure!

Glossary

Here are defined some basic terms that relate to adult children raising children. I hope they will encourage and challenge you to think deeply about these issues.

Acceptance: Personal acknowledgment of facts, events, feelings or other realities and the integration of these into your thinking so that you think and act harmoniously, as if these things were indeed so.

Addiction: A physical compulsion coupled with a mental obsession to consume a particular mood-altering chemical substance, created by a dynamic and progressive interplay between the toxicity of the substance and the victim's tolerance to it (sometimes extended to include compulsions not chemically based but used in its narrower meaning here).

Adult Child: An adult whose parent or primary caretaker in the childhood home suffered from addiction.

Al-Anon: An anonymous fellowship of relatives and friends of problem drinkers who share their experience, strength and hope in order to solve their common problem of reacting to the problem drinker. A 12-Step program originated by and for the families of AA members.

185

Alcoholic: One who is addicted to alcohol. In the current state of medical knowledge, there is no definitive test for diagnosis. Only the alcoholic knows when and if he has become addicted.

Alcoholics Anonymous: An anonymous fellowship of alcoholics who share their experience, strength and hope in order to help themselves to stop drinking. Founded by two alcoholics around 1940, it combines regular fellowship, inspirational reading and personal introspection, using the 12 Steps to Spiritual Enlightenment. It has been the model of thousands of groups worldwide and has been responsible for helping three-quarters of a million alcoholics to control their addiction.

Alcoholism: Addiction to alcohol. Alcohol is the most inexpensive, easily made, socially acceptable, frequently used and collectively destructive mood-altering chemical substance known. Compared with most other known addictive substances, however, its toxicity is relatively low in small quantities, allowing for significant tolerance to build up prior to the development of addiction.

Anger: The feeling you have when you cannot control some person or event that you would like to control.

Co-dependency: A process by which you live as if your happiness or well-being depended upon someone else's behavior and you direct your words and actions to try to control that behavior. Usually developed in response to someone who is chemically dependent or in a co-dependent pattern himself, the focus of co-dependency is transferable to another person who is not personally dependent, at least initially. Co-dependency is contagious, unlike primary dependency.

Communication: The sharing of thoughts and feelings with another by means of words, expressions, body language, signals or symbols.

Connectedness: The feeling of sharing a common purpose, belonging and being mutually valuable that you get from relating to others as spiritual equals.

Defenses: The use of words or actions to prevent another from making their point or accomplishing their immediate goal, which you perceive as a threat to your personal well-being or sense of self.

Dependency: Progressive reliance on a particular mood-altering chemical substance for your sense of well-being, caused by the need to relieve chronic physical or mental pain from the interplay of toxicity and tolerance with regard to that substance (synonymous with addiction as used here).

Despair: The feeling of abandonment and isolation you have when all self-esteem and spiritual connectedness are gone.

Dysfunctional: The state of being unable to carry out normal adult activities relating to self-care, self-support and family or household duties.

Family of choice: That physical, social and spiritual unit which you chose in your adult life for expression of human intimacy and reproduction.

Family of origin: That physical, social and spiritual unit in which you were born and which gave you early nurture.

Forgiveness: Acceptance of a person for his spiritual value regardless of his acts or words. The relinquishment of any right to judge another or yourself.

Guilt: The feeling that some action or inaction of yours in the past has made you permanently vulnerable and obligated.

Independence: The quality of being self-determining, taking responsibility for yourself and your destiny and finding contentment doing so. Freedom from dependency for your happiness or well-being on any particular person, group or thing to supervise, control or approve your words or actions.

Judgment: The act of decision about whether some person or thing is right or wrong, good or evil. Since all things can be used for right or wrong and all people have some goodness, it is impossible and fruitless to judge anyone or anything except with direct reference to what is right and good for you. Your judgment, then, affects only you, not those you would judge.

Love: Finding the good in a person, place or thing and enjoying it. It is a celebration, best communicated to the loved one but always independent of the response.

Manipulation: The use of words or actions to shift someone else's immediate goals in order to meet your personal goals.

Parent-child bond: The natural, indestructible physiological and psychological link between parent and child resulting from shared genetics, experience and emotional resonance.

Rage: Anger detached from any particular person or event.

Recovery: The process of liberating yourself from dependency on any particular substance or from co-dependency on any particular person or event for your personal well-being. It is accomplished by acceptance of your innate spiritual value and by cultivation of your serenity through spiritual connectedness.

Rejection: The feeling of abandonment and unworthiness that you feel when someone you love fails to give you the attention you want.

Relationship: The multi-leveled link that two or a group of people create together when each projects energy in the direction of the other and each feels some payoff.

Self-esteem: Your sense of self with respect to your inherent value and life-purpose as a human being in relation to others and the universe.

Serenity: The state of being at peace with yourself, a state in which you have sole control over your personal happiness.

Shame: Guilt that has become detached from any particular action or inaction in the past.

Spiritual: Relating to that part of life that is under the control of a power greater than ourselves or than any other known physical force and which interconnects us at the level of mind.

Spirituality: That quality of life which interconnects us at the level of mind and manifests in each individual creation as a piece of a larger whole.

12-Step
Program: A program for personal growth through self-knowledge, based on the 12 Steps to Spiritual Enlightenment adopted by Alcoholics Anonymous and Al-Anon which originated in the Oxford Group over a century ago as a distillation of spiritual truth from many traditions. It combines work on the Steps, regular fellowship and inspirational reading and puts special focus on living in the present, one day at a time.

Universal reality: The intuitively knowable and logically irreducible bundle of relationships on the physical, mental and spiritual levels that has no exception. For our purposes, it can be perceived in the present time and place only, freed of the past and unlimited for the future.

Validation: The process by which someone feels loved. It is an affirmation of one's basic goodness and value.

Recommended
Reading

Adult Children

Bradshaw, John. **Bradshaw On: The Family**. Deerfield Beach, FL: Health Communications, 1988.

Friel, John and Friel, Linda. **Adult Children: The Secrets Of Dysfunctional Families**. Deerfield Beach, FL: Health Communications, 1988.

Lerner, Rokelle. **Daily Affirmations**. Deerfield Beach, FL: Health Communications, 1985.

Somers, Suzanne. **Keeping Secrets**. New York: Warner Books, 1988.

Woititz, Janet. **Adult Children Of Alcoholics**. Deerfield Beach, FL: Health Communications, 1983.

——————. **Struggle For Intimacy**. Deerfield Beach, FL: Health Communications, 1985.

Co-dependency

Al-Anon Staff. **One Day At A Time in Al-Anon**. New York: Al-Anon, 1986.

Beattie, Melody. **Co-dependent No More**. Center City, MN: Hazelden, 1987.

Co-dependency. (An Anthology) Deerfield Beach, FL: Health Communications, 1988.

Forward, Susan and Torres, Joan. **Men Who Hate Women And The Women Who Love Them**. New York: Bantam, 1986.

Miller, Joy. **Addictive Relationships: Reclaiming Your Boundaries**. Deerfield Beach, FL: Health Communications, 1989.

Norwood, Robin. **Women Who Love Too Much.** New York: Pocket Books, 1986.

Subby, Robert. **Lost In The Shuffle: The Co-dependent Reality.** Deerfield Beach, FL: Health Communications, 1987.

Wegscheider-Cruse, Sharon. **Choicemaking.** Deerfield Beach, FL: Health Communications, 1985.

Whitfield, Charles. **Healing The Child Within.** Deerfield Beach, FL: Health Communications, 1987.

Addiction

Beasley, Joseph. **Wrong Diagnosis - Wrong Treatment: An Alcoholic's Plight.** Durant, OK: Creative Infomatics, 1987.

Goodwin, Donald. **Is Alcoholism Hereditary?** New York: OUP, 1976.

Robertson, Nan. **Getting Better.** New York: William Morrow, 1988.

Personal Growth And Self-Help

Benson, Herbert and Klipper, Miriam. **The Relaxation Response.** New York: Avon, 1976.

Clance, Pauline. **The Imposter Phenomenom: Overcoming The Fear That Haunts Your Success.** Atlanta, GA: Peachtree, 1985.

Dyer, Wayne. **Your Erroneous Zones.** New York: Avon, 1977.

Fromm, Erich. **The Art Of Loving.** New York: Harper and Row, 1974.

Harris, Thomas A. **I'm OK, You're OK.** New York: Avon, 1982.

James, Muriel and Jongewald, Dorothy. **Born To Win: Transactional Analysis With Gestalt Experiments.** New York: NAL, 1978.

Judson, Stephanie, ed. **A Manual On Nonviolence And Children.** Philadelphia, PA: New Society, 1984.

Maslow, Abraham. **Motivation And Personality.** New York: Harper and Row, 1970.

Parents Anonymous. **I Am A Parents Anonymous Parent.** Los Angeles, CA: Parents Anonymous.

Rogers, Carl R. **On Becoming A Person.** Boston, MA: Houghton-Mifflin, 1961.

Parenting

Bettelheim, Bruno. **Dialogues With Mothers.** New York: Free Press, 1962.

Briggs, Dorothy. **Your Child's Self-Esteem - The Key To His Life.** New York: Doubleday, 1975.

Campbell, Ross. **How To Really Love Your Child.** New York: NAL, 1982.

Crary, Elizabeth. **Without Spanking Or Spoiling.** Seattle, WA: Parenting Press, 1979.

Daley, Eliot. **Father Feelings.** New York: Pocket Books, 1979.

Dodson, Fitzhugh. **How To Parent.** New York: NAL, 1973.

Dyer, Wayne. **What Do You Really Want For Your Children?** New York: Avon, 1986.

Faber, Adele and Mazlish, Elaine. **How To Talk So Kids Will Listen And Listen So Kids Will Talk.** New York: Avon, 1982.

Ginott, Haim. **Between Parent And Child.** New York: Avon, 1969.

Greenspan, Stanley and Greenspan, Nancy. **First Feelings.** New York: Penguin, 1986.

Leman, Kevin. **The Birth Order Book.** New York: Dell, 1987.

Pruett, Kyle. **The Nurturing Father.** New York: Warner Books, 1988.

Rogers, Fred and Head, Barry. **Mister Rogers Talks With Parents.** New York: Berkeley, 1986.

Rolfe, Randy. **You Can Postpone Anything But Love.** Edgemont, PA: Ambassador Press, 1985; New York: Warner Books, forthcoming.

Learning And Education

Bateson, Gregory. **Mind And Nature: A Necessary Unity.** New York: Bantam, 1988.

——————. **Steps To An Ecology Of The Mind.** New York: Ballantine, 1975.

Bloom, Alan. **The Closing Of The American Mind.** New York: Simon and Schuster, 1987.

Holt, John. **How Children Learn.** New York: Dell, 1923.

——————. **Why Children Fail.** New York: Dell, 1988.

Kozol, Jonathan. **Illiterate America.** New York: NAL, 1986.

——————. **Death At An Early Age.** New York: NAL, 1986.

Neill, A.S. **Summerhill: A Radical Approach To Child Rearing.** New York: Pocket Books, 1984.

Shilcock, Susan and Bergson, Peter A. **Open Connections: The Other Basics.** Bryn Mawr: Open Connections, 1980.

Family Life And Choices

Cahill, Mary Ann. **The Heart Has Its Own Reasons.** New York: NAL, 1985.

Crook, William G. and Stevens, Laura J. **Solving The Puzzle Of Your Hard To Raise Child.** New York: Random House, 1987.

Dick-Read, Grantly. **Childbirth Without Fear.** New York: Harper and Row, 1984.

Elkind, David. **The Hurried Child: Growing Up Too Fast Too Soon.** Reading, MA: Addison-Wesley, 1981.

Fraiberg, Selma. "Every Child's Birthright." In **Selected Writings Of Selma Fraiberg,** ed. Louis Fraiberg. Columbus, OH: Ohio State University Press, 1987.

Holt, John. **Teach Your Own: A New And Hopeful Path For Parents And Educators.** New York: Dell, 1982.

Judson, Stephanie, ed. **A Manual On Nonviolence And Children.** Philadelphia, PA: New Society, 1984.

Leboyer, Frederick. **Birth Without Violence.** New York: Knopf, 1975.

Kippley, Sheila. **Breastfeeding And Natural Child Spacing.** New York: Penguin, 1975.

Lappe, Frances Moore. **What To Do After You Turn Off The TV.** New York: Ballantine, 1985.

Macy, Joanna R. **Despair And Personal Power In The Nuclear Age.** Philadelphia, PA: New Society, 1983.

Moynihan, Daniel Patrick. **Family And Nation.** San Diego, CA: Harcourt Brace Jovanovich, 1986.

Thevenin, Tine. **The Family Bed.** Garden City Park, NY: Avery, 1987.

Torgus, Judy, ed. **The Womanly Art Of Breastfeeding.** La Leche League International, 1987.

Spirituality And Inspiration

Capra, Fritjof. **The Tao Of Physics.** New York: Bantam, 1984.

Emerson, Ralph Waldo. **Emerson's Essays.** New York: Harper and Row, 1981.

Fulghum, Robert. **All I Really Needed To Know I Learned In Kindergarten.** New York: Random House, 1988.

Gawain, Shakti. **Creative Visualization.** San Rafael, CA: New World Library, 1978.

Greeley, Andrew. **The Patience Of A Saint.** New York: Warner Books, 1986.

Hay, Louise. **You Can Heal Your Life.** Santa Monica, CA: Hay House, 1984.

Jampolsky, Gerald et al. **Good-Bye To Guilt: Releasing Fear Through Forgiveness.** New York: Bantam, 1985.

Kushner, Harold. **When All You've Ever Wanted Isn't Enough.** Boston, MA: G. K. Hall, 1987.

Nearing, Helen and Nearing, Scott. **Living The Good Life: How To Live Sanely And Simply In A Troubled World.** New York: Schocken Books, 1971.

Peale, Norman Vincent. **The Power Of Positive Thinking.** New York: Prentice-Hall, 1954.

Peck, M. Scott. **The Road Less Travelled.** New York: Simon and Schuster, 1980.

Powers, Thomas E. **Invitation To A Great Experiment.** Hankins, NY: East Ridge Press, 1986.

Schuller, Robert. **Tough Times Never Last, But Tough People Do.** Nashville, TN: Nelson, 1983.

Siegel, Bernie. **Love, Medicine And Miracles.** New York: Harper and Row, 1988.

Teilhard de Chardin, Pierre. **The Phenomenon of Man.** New York: Harper and Row, 1959.

Watts, Alan W. **The Way Of Zen.** New York: Random House, 1974.

Wright, Robert. **Three Scientists And Their Gods.** New York: Time Books, 1988.

Mind And Language

Chomsky, Noam. **Reflections On Language.** New York: Pantheon, 1975.

Freud, Sigmund. **The Basic Writings Of Sigmund Freud.** New York: Modern Library, 1938.

Jaynes, Julian. **The Origin Of Consciousness In The Breakdown Of The Bicameral Mind..** Boston, MA: Houghton-Mifflin, 1977.

Jung, Carl. **The Basic Writings Of Carl Jung.** Ed. by Violet S. De Laslzo. New York: Modern Library, 1959.

Piaget, Jean. **The Language And Thought Of A Child.** New York: NAL, 1955.

Rico, Gabriele L. **Writing The Natural Way: Using Right-Brain Techniques To Release Your Expressive Powers.** Los Angeles, CA: J. P. Tarcher, 1983.

Wolf, Fred A. **Star Wave: Mind, Consciousness And Quantum Physics.** New York: Macmillan, 1986.

Cultural Anthropology

Eisler, Riane. **The Chalice And The Blade: Our History, Our Future.** New York: Harper and Row, 1987.

Kitzinger, Sheila. **Women As Mothers.** New York: Random House, 1979.

Leakey, Richard and Lewin, Roger. **Origins: What New Discoveries Reveal About The Emergence Of Our Species And Its Possible Future.** New York: Dutton, 1982.

Mead, Margaret. **Cooperation And Competition Among Primitive Peoples.** Magnolia, MA: Peter Smith.

Montagu, Ashley. **The Nature Of Human Aggression.** New York: OUP, 1976.

_____. **Touching: The Human Significance Of The Skin.** New York: Harper and Row, 1971.

Books from . . .
Health Communications

AFTER THE TEARS: Reclaiming The Personal Losses of Childhood
Jane Middelton-Moz and Lorie Dwinnel
Your lost childhood must be grieved in order for you to recapture your
self-worth and enjoyment of life. This book will show you how.
ISBN 0-932194-36-2   **$7.95**

HEALING YOUR SEXUAL SELF
Janet Woititz
How can you break through the aftermath of sexual abuse and enter into
healthy relationships? Survivors are shown how to recognize the problem
and deal effectively with it.
ISBN 1-55874-018-X   **$7.95**

RECOVERY FROM RESCUING
Jacqueline Castine
Effective psychological and spiritual principles teach you when to take
charge, when to let go, and how to break the cycle of guilt and fear that
keeps you in the responsibility trap. Mind-altering ideas and exercises will
guide you to a more carefree life.
ISBN 1-55874-016-3   **$7.95**

ADDICTIVE RELATIONSHIPS: Reclaiming Your Boundaries
Joy Miller
We have given ourselves away to spouse, lover, children, friends or
parents. By examining where we are, where we want to go and how to get
there, we can reclaim our personal boundaries and the true love of
ourselves.
ISBN 1-55874-003-1   **$7.95**

RECOVERY FROM CO-DEPENDENCY:
It's Never Too Late To Reclaim Your Childhood
Laurie Weiss, Jonathan B. Weiss
Having been brought up with life-repressing decisions, the adult child
recognizes something isn't working. This book shows how to change
decisions and live differently and fully.
ISBN 0-932194-85-0   **$9.95**

SHIPPING/HANDLING: All orders shipped UPS unless weight exceeds 200 lbs., special routing is requested, or
delivery territory is outside continental U.S. Orders outside United States shipped either Air Parcel Post or Surface
Parcel Post. Shipping and handling charges apply to all orders shipped whether UPS, Book Rate, Library Rate, Air
or Surface Parcel Post or Common Carrier and will be charged as follows. Orders less than $25.00 in value add
$2.00 minimum. Orders from $25.00 to $50.00 in value (after discount) add $2.50 minimum. Orders greater than
$50.00 in value (after discount) add 6% of value. Orders greater than $25.00 outside United States add 15% of
value. We are not responsible for loss or damage unless material is shipped UPS. Allow 3-5 weeks after receipt of
order for delivery. Prices are subject to change without prior notice.

Enterprise Center, 3201 S.W. 15th Street,
Deerfield Beach, FL 33442
1-800-851-9100

Health
Communications, Inc.

Other Books By . . .
Health Communications

ADULT CHILDREN OF ALCOHOLICS
Janet Woititz
Over a year on *The New York Times* Best-Seller list, this book is the primer on Adult Children of Alcoholics.
ISBN 0-932194-15-X $6.95

STRUGGLE FOR INTIMACY
Janet Woititz
Another best-seller, this book gives insightful advice on learning to love more fully.
ISBN 0-932194-25-7 $6.95

DAILY AFFIRMATIONS: For Adult Children of Alcoholics
Rokelle Lerner
These positive affirmations for every day of the year paint a mental picture of your life as you choose it to be.
ISBN 0-932194-27-3 $6.95

CHOICEMAKING: For Co-dependents, Adult Children and Spirituality Seekers — Sharon Wegscheider-Cruse
This useful book defines the problems and solves them in a positive way.
ISBN 0-932194-26-5 $9.95

LEARNING TO LOVE YOURSELF: Finding Your Self-Worth
Sharon Wegscheider-Cruse
"Self-worth is a choice, not a birthright," says the author as she shows us how we can choose positive self-esteem.
ISBN 0-932194-39-7 $7.95

BRADSHAW ON: THE FAMILY: A Revolutionary Way of Self-Discovery
John Bradshaw
The host of the nationally televised series of the same name shows us how families can be healed and individuals can realize full potential.
ISBN 0-932194-54-0 $9.95

HEALING THE CHILD WITHIN:
Discovery and Recovery for Adult Children of Dysfunctional Families
Charles Whitfield
Dr. Whitfield defines, describes and discovers how we can reach our Child Within to heal and nurture our woundedness.
ISBN 0-932194-40-0 $8.95

Enterprise Center, 3201 S.W. 15th Street,
Deerfield Beach, FL 33442
1-800-851-9100

Health Communications, Inc.

Daily Affirmation Books from . . .
Health Communications

GENTLE REMINDERS FOR CO-DEPENDENTS: Daily Affirmations
Mitzi Chandler
With insight and humor, Mitzi Chandler takes the co-dependent and the
adult child through the year. Gentle Reminders is for those in recovery
who seek to enjoy the miracle each day brings.
ISBN 1-55874-020-1   **$6.95**

TIME FOR JOY: Daily Affirmations
Ruth Fishel
With quotations, thoughts and healing energizing affirmations these daily
messages address the fears and imperfections of being human, guiding us
through self-acceptance to a tangible peace and the place within where
there is *time for joy.*
ISBN 0-932194-82-6   **$6.95**

CRY HOPE: Positive Affirmations For Healthy Living
Jan Veltman
This book gives positive daily affirmations for seekers and those in
recovery. Every day is a new adventure, and change is a challenge.
ISBN 0-932194-74-5   **$6.95**

SAY YES TO LIFE: Daily Affirmations For Recovery
Father Leo Booth
These meditations take you through the year day by day with Father Leo
Booth, looking for answers and sometimes discovering that there are
none. Father Leo tells us, "For the recovering compulsive person God is
too important to miss — may you find Him now."
IBN 0-932194-46-X   **$6.95**

DAILY AFFIRMATIONS: For Adult Children of Alcoholics
Rokelle Lerner
Affirmations are a way to discover personal awareness, growth and
spiritual potential, and self-regard. Reading this book gives us an
opportunity to nurture ourselves, learn who we are and what we want to
become.
ISBN 0-932194-47-3
(Little Red Book)   **$6.95**
(New Cover Edition)   **$6.95**

Enterprise Center, 3201 S.W. 15th Street,
Deerfield Beach, FL 33442
1-800-851-9100

Health Communications, Inc.